ADHD MONEY

A Finance Book Made for
Your Neurodivergent Brain

ADHD MONEY

Tina Mathams
The ADHD Accountant

WILEY

First published 2025 by John Wiley & Sons Australia, Ltd

© John Wiley & Sons Australia, Ltd 2025

All rights reserved, including rights for text and data mining and training of artificial intelligence technologies or similar technologies. Except as permitted under the *Australian Copyright Act 1968* (for example, a fair dealing for the purposes of study, research, criticism or review) no part of this publication may be reproduced, stored in a retrieval system, or transmitted, in any form or by any means, electronic, mechanical, photocopying, recording or otherwise. Advice on how to obtain permission to reuse material from this title is available at http://www.wiley.com/go/permissions.

The right of Tina Mathams to be identified as the author of *ADHD Money* has been asserted in accordance with law.

ISBN: 978-1-394-28077-3

A catalogue record for this book is available from the National Library of Australia

Registered Office
John Wiley & Sons Australia, Ltd. Level 4, 600 Bourke Street, Melbourne, VIC 3000, Australia

For details of our global editorial offices, customer services, and more information about Wiley products visit us at www.wiley.com.

Wiley also publishes its books in a variety of electronic formats and by print-on-demand. Some content that appears in standard print versions of this book may not be available in other formats.

Trademarks: Wiley and the Wiley logo are trademarks or registered trademarks of John Wiley & Sons, Inc. and/or its affiliates in the United States and other countries and may not be used without written permission. All other trademarks are the property of their respective owners. John Wiley & Sons, Inc. is not associated with any product or vendor mentioned in this book.

Limit of Liability/Disclaimer of Warranty
While the publisher and author have used their best efforts in preparing this work, they make no representations or warranties with respect to the accuracy or completeness of the contents of this work and specifically disclaim all warranties, including without limitation any implied warranties of merchantability or fitness for a particular purpose. No warranty may be created or extended by sales representatives, written sales materials or promotional statements for this work. This work is sold with the understanding that the publisher is not engaged in rendering professional services. The advice and strategies contained herein may not be suitable for your situation. You should consult with a specialist where appropriate. The fact that an organisation, website, or product is referred to in this work as a citation and/or potential source of further information does not mean that the publisher and author endorse the information or services the organisation, website, or product may provide or recommendations it may make. Further, readers should be aware that websites listed in this work may have changed or disappeared between when this work was written and when it is read. Neither the publisher nor author shall be liable for any loss of profit or any other commercial damages, including but not limited to special, incidental, consequential, or other damages.

Cover design by Alissa Dinalo
Images: Symbols/icons: © artnazu / Adobe Stock; Piggy bank: © Vector Vista / Adobe Stock; Mason jar: © Kateryna / Adobe Stock; Christmas tree/car: © salim138 / Adobe Stock; Suitcase: © Poscdode / Adobe Stock

Set in 11.5/14.5 pts and Americane by Straive, Chennai, India.

SKYFF107287-13F0-4D00-9C86-C775DC20C824_062725

*To my husband, who has fiercely encouraged me and
kept me accountable.*

*To my kids, who completely changed my life. Without them,
all of this wouldn't have been possible.*

*To the neurodivergent community, who are trusting me to help you with
your finances: thank you. I hope this book gives you the dopamine you
need to live your financial life on your own terms.*

Contents

About the Author ix
Introduction: Welcome to ADHD Money xi
Glossary xix

1 Understanding ADHD and Money   1
2 Navigating Emotions and Money   29
3 Reframing Your Money Mindset   63
4 Managing Your Expenses   95
5 The ADHD Spending Plan   119
6 Tools and Strategies to Keep the Novelty Alive   139
7 Saving Money and Paying Off Debt   163
8 Setting Achievable Goals   193
9 Frequently Asked Questions   205

Conclusion: The Dessert Menu 215

About the Author

Tina Mathams is a qualified accountant, a financial educator and the founder of Diverse Accountants, ADHD Money and the *ADHD Money and Finance* podcast. Tina is an in-demand speaker in the neurodivergent community, offering her insights and knowledge into how neurodivergent people can live a financially healthier life.

Tina has been featured on many podcasts and has worked with organisations such as Commonwealth Bank. She creates content and courses designed to be easily accessible to those who feel that typical financial advice has not worked for them in the past.

Tina lives in Brisbane, Australia, with her husband, two kids, two cats and one Dachshund. In her spare time, she enjoys re-watching her favourite comfort shows, going to the arcade with her kids, going out to eat with her family and indulging in her latest hyperfixation.

INTRODUCTION

Welcome to *ADHD Money*

You are not bad with money

You just haven't learned yet how to work *with* your brain, rather than against it, when it comes to finances.

This book has been written for the ADHD brain. Being neurodivergent myself, I know we can get bored easily, need novelty, have brains that jump around and we might not be able to sit still for too long. So you can either go chapter by chapter or jump to certain chapters that interest you more.

I've ensured that you can write in this book, use sticky notes in it and even highlight words, activities or concepts that are important to you or that you might want to revisit later. It's a workbook rather than a novel.

I specifically designed it this way, so you don't get lost in too many words if you have trouble reading — or if you get bored easily. Along the way, I will also give you actionable steps. So you won't get to the end and think '*What now*?'

I know that we can often read something, get excited to implement change and then lose traction once we have gotten that dopamine hit (more on that later). I encourage you not to try to implement *everything* in this book all at once.

Rather, take one step, then another, then another ... until you have built on your knowledge and skills. *This* is where you will see change in how you feel about money and your overall financial wellness.

Consistency is key.

Nah, just kidding! (And I hope your heart rate is OK.) You and I both know that ADHDers are anything but *typically* consistent. Let that be OK. We are neuroaffirming here.

Being *persistent*, not consistent, is where the party is at. If you are persistent in the pursuit of your financial wellness, you will achieve it. And the secret to being persistent is building some self-trust, knowing you aren't a failure if you aren't consistent, and believing that you are a financial badass. So let's get to it.

Who am I?

My name is Tina, and I am the founder of ADHD Money and Diverse Accountants. I have been diagnosed with AuDHD (autism and ADHD), I'm an accountant, financial educator, wife, mother and cat lover. I love Formula 1, the paranormal and history. Did I mention I love cats?

I have loved numbers for as long as I can remember. When I was seven, I would do maths equations on repeat. I'd happily sit there for what seemed like hours figuring out the sums.

I like to try and be funny (note: *try*) so I sprinkle a bit of humour throughout this book. If it's not your type of humour, or you have no idea what my brain is doing ... then just move on, it's fine. A lot of the time, I have no idea what my brain is doing either.

A little note to send you off into your future of financial wellness: everyone is different. Even each ADHDer. We're neurodivergent, not robots.

How to use this book

This book has been developed through:

- my knowledge from my professional life
- my knowledge of ADHD
- my knowledge from working with or talking to thousands of ADHD adults
- my knowledge from working with a neuroaffirming counsellor for the last few years.

My goal has been to create a really handy, practical resource that will help others like me to sort out their money mess. The tips and strategies for managing your money will be handy and useful for a lot of people — but especially for those who are neurodivergent.

That said, this book is not a diagnostic tool. Just because you find *ADHD Money* useful, it doesn't mean you *must* have ADHD. Lots of people find that the 'typical' money advice doesn't work for them. Those people, neurodivergent or not, might want to try the tools and ideas shared in this book.

It's important to remember that neurodivergence is a spectrum. My hope is that you find everything in this book helpful, but it's much more likely that there might be some things that don't suit you — and that's OK. Take what suits you, and leave the rest.

This is also not a medical guide. I'm going to repeat this a few times throughout: if you need more help to implement these strategies, or just more help generally, then your GP, a specialist or a good therapist can help you explore the challenges you're facing.

So what *will* you find in *ADHD Money*? I hope you'll discover how to get comfortable with your finances and manage your money more effectively. Ultimately, I hope you'll find a new sense of financial empowerment.

We'll look at how your brain, your emotions, your mindset and your values all influence your relationship with money. We'll touch on common money topics like spending, expenses, cash flow, savings and debt.

We'll also get into some strategies to help your ADHD brain stay engaged, interested and motivated.

And throughout the book, you'll uncover information, resources and activities, including worksheets and trackers. These will help you take action.

If you don't want to write in the book but you have a journal or notepad you like, you can follow the exercises that way instead.

And as you go, if one chapter doesn't resonate with you, you can skip to another that feels more urgent. You never know, what you leave now, you might come back to later. That's the funny thing with humans. Our lives change and sometimes what we needed before is not what we need now or in the future.

I'm so excited to bring you this book, and I hope you reference it for years to come.

You are not bad with money. You just haven't learned yet how to work *with* your brain, rather than against it.

Been there, done that, got the ADHD postcard

You will read bits of my story throughout the book, but I'll share a bit more for you here.

Throughout school, my special interest remained maths and numbers, with a bit of writing thrown in for good measure. While I had lots of ideas of what I'd want to do when I grew up, a business degree seemed like a natural fit for me. I started majoring in economics but switched to an accounting major.

I always thought I was bad with money. Being an accountant, you can bet I kept that to myself. I remember when I got my first credit card while at university, I thought I'd be smart with it and just use it for things I needed. This was back in the *olden days* (circa 2004) when debit cards for online purchasing were hard to come by. You had to have savings (ha!) or earn a certain amount to be eligible for one. So, I settled on a credit card instead, so that I could buy a magazine subscription. Yes, that was actually my motivation for getting a credit card.

Side note: how funny that it was so much easier to get a credit card (debt) than a debit card (your own money)! The banking regulations have come a long way, my friend.

Anyway, I think you can imagine how that turned out. I was not responsible with my credit card. I bought all the things, and I only paid the minimum repayment each month. I shudder to think how much money I accumulated in interest. It was years before I got it all paid off, and I'm sure it was only a $2000 limit.

I like to tell stories of my previous less-than-desirable financial management so you know the person educating and guiding you about money is someone who has been there and done that. I get it. I know how challenging money management can be. I used to shame myself for being *'terrible'* with money. I'd feel guilty for spending beyond my means.

When I found out I had ADHD, I put two and two together and it all started to make sense.

At this time, I was posting on my Instagram account @theadhdaccountant. I started posting about ADHD and money, and I was floored by how many people resonated with my content and story. From there, ADHD Money was born.

I wanted to make the neurodivergent community feel better about their finances and look at their money through a completely different lens. This book is for all of you who have made that possible and who have resonated with my story, and those of you who are wanting to manage your money on your own terms! You *can* do this.

Glossary

ADHD (Attention Deficit Hyperactivity Disorder): ADHD is a neurodevelopmental condition that affects executive functioning and can cause inattention, impulsivity and hyperactivity.

Avalanche Method: A method that involves paying the debts with the highest interest rates first.

Body Doubling: When you and another person (or people!) get together and work through something you need to do.

Cash Flow: The movement of money in and out of your bank accounts.

Debt Challenge: Similar to a savings challenge, a fun way to gamify paying down debt.

Emotional Dysregulation: A difficulty in managing and controlling emotional responses. Emotional dysregulation can involve intense, prolonged and/or inappropriate emotional reactions in everyday situations.

Emotional Spending: Occurs when we let our emotions drive our money decisions.

Executive Functioning: The brain's command centre. Executive functioning can include: planning, prioritising, impulse control, self-monitoring, focus.

Financial Values: Core values that align with your financial choices.

Gamifying: The use of elements and principles of game design to make other activities more engaging. Also called gamification.

Habit Stacking: The process of pairing a task that you need or want to do with a habit you already do and enjoy.

Impulse Spending: To spend money without really thinking it through.

Interest-Based Nervous System: A nervous system that only focusses on things of interest.

Savings Challenge: A fun way to gamify your savings.

Self-Regulation: Activities or actions you take to keep cool and calm when you're stressed or feeling dysregulated.

Snowball Method: A method that involves paying off the smallest debt first, which then 'snowballs' into paying off the bigger debts.

CHAPTER 1
Understanding ADHD and Money

In this chapter we get into...

- How and why ADHD can impact your money management
- Your brain's strengths
- Your interest-based nervous system (and why it struggles with money)
- Key motivation factors for the ADHD brain
- Recognising what you like (and maybe don't like) about money

How I became 'the ADHD Accountant'

When I was first diagnosed with ADHD, one of my first thoughts was, 'Can I still be an accountant?' I even Googled if ADHD and being an accountant were compatible!

Much of what I'd read about ADHD was how much we struggle with everything. Things like organisation, prioritisation, emotional management and, of course, money management. I wasn't sure how that could work with my job.

I started my Instagram account (@theadhdaccountant) because I had so many people ask for help. This confirmed for me I really wasn't alone — that many people with ADHD run into difficulties when it comes to managing their finances.

What did people ask? Among the most common questions were things like:

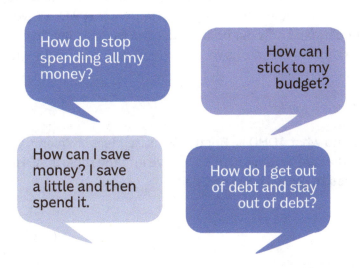

A part of me felt like a fraud. I, too, had my fair share of financial mismanagement in my time. I'd spent beyond my means. I'd been in consumer debt. I had started budgets but failed to stick to them.

However, I could easily help others manage their money. Something I'd done in my work as an accountant. I'd help businesses manage their budgets and forecasts, so why did I have so much trouble with my own finances?

This is something that is very typical in the ADHD world. We can do something that we struggle doing for ourselves quite easily for someone else.

Anyway, in among all this internal dialogue I realised I'd come a long way in my financial management from 15–20 years ago. The strategies I'd tried and tested, and ultimately put into place, had gotten me from financial ruin, to doing financially OK.

This led me into a hyperfocus on ADHD and finances. I wanted to really understand the link between two subjects that usually don't co-exist. Coupling this with my training and experience as an accountant, I worked with other neurodivergent people to help them too. What I learned was eye-opening!

For decades and across the world, ADHDers have proclaimed they are bad with money. But are we? Are we bad with money? Or do we just need to understand how our brain works and manage our finances in a neurodivergent way? Perhaps we just need a way that works with our brain rather than against it?

Spoiler alert: it's the latter.

Let's dive into what ADHD is. Briefly. Because there are plenty of resources that are better equipped to dive into the topic of ADHD itself; plus we need to get to the money part.

Attentive Deficit Hyperactivity Disorder (ADHD)

If you are reading this book, I assume you have heard of ADHD. You either have been diagnosed or identify as neurodivergent, or love someone who is neurodivergent. Whatever your relationship, you are welcome here and thank you for picking up this colourful and nothing-like-you-have-seen-before book.

ADHD is a neurodevelopmental condition that affects executive functioning and can cause inattention, impulsivity and hyperactivity. There are also emotional regulation and working memory challenges associated with ADHD.

Some of the challenges of ADHD can include:

- regulating attention
- regulating emotions
- being forgetful
- finding it difficult to organise tasks, time and belongings
- finding it hard to sit
- losing belongings
- struggling to follow through on instructions
- interrupting others
- being impulsive
- not being able to tolerate boredom.

That's just a short list of what someone with ADHD can struggle with day to day. It's not exhaustive and not diagnostic.

While there can be ways to help manage ADHD, it's a condition that most people will carry through their lifetime.

Of course, there are some amazing qualities people with ADHD can have. Again, this is not a complete list, but we have a few goodies to balance the not-so-great parts.

- We tend to be great in an emergency.
- We can have lots of ideas and be very creative.
- We can hyperfocus on topics that we are interested in.
- We can often think outside the box and see things that others cannot.
- We are resilient.
- We can have a lot of energy.

SIDEQUEST

The amazing ADHD brain

Rather than focus on what we struggle with when it comes to ADHD and money, take some time to focus on the amazing qualities we have. Some of our strengths and skills can be really beneficial when it comes to managing money.

- Which of the strengths on the next page do you relate to the most?
- Can you think of any personal strengths you might have?

ADHD strengths and skills

Feature	Description
Great in an emergency	We can focus our attention, process information quickly and act fast when the pressure's on.
Highly creative	We are full of big ideas and have a flair for the unexpected.
Hyperfocused	We are passionate and know lots about what matters most to us.
Able to think outside the box	We come at things from different angles, and sometimes we can see solutions other people miss.
Resilient	We're adaptable, and we can bounce back from setbacks or disappointments stronger than ever.
High energy levels	We have lots of oomph and enthusiasm to fuel our work, life and dreams.

The ADHD brain and the interest-based nervous system

ADHDers operate on an **interest-based nervous system**. Simply put, that means we often struggle to focus on things that don't grab our interest. While neurotypical people might be motivated by outcomes or rewards, we are generally motivated by what we find fascinating or enjoyable in the moment.

An interest-based nervous system is one reason we often prefer to research the subject of our latest hyperfocus rather than do the dishes — even though we know the dishes need to be done. It's not as simple as just telling ourselves 'hey, the dishes are important'.

The interest-based nervous system

With an interest-based nervous system, an ADHD brain is motivated by four key factors:

- interest
- novelty
- urgency
- challenge.

As these four factors suggest, our brains like to prioritise tasks or activities that are engaging, exciting or rewarding. If a task involves some degree of interest, novelty, challenge and/or urgency, the ADHD brain is more likely to want to see it through.

So what does an interest-based nervous system mean for you when it comes to money?

This need to feel interest, novelty, urgency or challenge is one reason you might find yourself avoiding things like budgeting or reviewing your spending. Those activities may not be engaging for your brain when there is no immediate reward.

People who are not neurodivergent can find it difficult to wrap their head around this, and it's one reason they might see ADHDers as 'lazy'.

But we are not lazy!

We just need to work with an interest-based nervous system, rather than against it.

The consequence-based nervous system

By comparison, a neurotypical brain will generally respond to the promise of possible outcomes. This is known as a **consequence-based nervous system**.

What motivates behaviour with this nervous system? It might be a fear of punishment or the promise of a reward. For example, the fear of potentially running out of money can be enough motivation for someone to check on their finances. Or they might think, 'If I budget, then I will have money for everything I need.'

In this way, someone with a consequence-based nervous system can usually work well with a sequence of tasks. They are motivated to follow that sequence of tasks (like budgeting) by the promise of the end result (having, or not having, money later).

It's time to find strategies that work for you.

If you find you shaming yourself for not being able to do the things that your nervous system literally doesn't allow you to do, I hope this brings you some peace and clarity. ADHDers can absolutely still prioritise and do all the things we need to for a more financially secure future. We just need to leverage our interest-based nervous system!

Our brains like to prioritise tasks or activities that are engaging, exciting or rewarding.

ADHD brain motivation factors

Throughout this book, I aim to challenge you to look outside the neurotypical finance box and use the **motivation factors** that work for the ADHD brain: interest, novelty, urgency and challenge.

You'll notice that I've called the activities throughout the book *challenges*. That's because they are important, and better yet, they're achievable. You've got this!

I also invite you to think about what might spark your *interest* when it comes to your financial management.

We'll look for *novelty* that you can put in place to help you smash your money goals.

And we'll find the *urgency* that will help motivate you.

ADHD motivation factors

Motivation factor	Description	Strategies to stay on track
Interest	We are stimulated by activities or topics that interest us personally.	Partner obligations with passions.
Novelty	We are drawn to new experiences and things that pique our curiosity.	Change it up.
Urgency	We act under pressure because we are driven by a time limit or a deadline.	Create your own urgency.
Challenge	We rise to a challenge that has a defined goal, an end point and, especially, a reward.	Give yourself rewards along the way. Find the why.

Strategies to help you stay motivated

Here are some examples of how you can put these motivation factors into practice.

- **Interest: Partner your obligations with passions**

    Think about what might spark your *interest* when it comes to your financial management. You can pair something that doesn't interest you with something you enjoy. For example, I often use what I do on the weekend as an example of this. I pop a podcast in my ears while I do my housework. This means I can do something I enjoy at the same time as I start a task I don't particularly enjoy.

- **Novelty: Change it up**

    Try doing an old task in a new way: in a new place, with different people, or using a new tool or method. For example, if you don't like tracking your **cash flow**, you could try doing it in a new environment, like your favourite café, or with a new tool, like an app.

- **Urgency: Create your own urgency**

    Focus on creating a sense of urgency that will help motivate you. You could implement your own deadlines, break big tasks down into smaller deadlines, or set a timer when doing an activity, for example, for things like bills that are before the actual due date. This can create some motivation before you need to pay it. (Use this one with caution; you don't want to get overly anxious.)

- **Challenge: Give yourself rewards along the way**

    If you can break the task down into chunks, you can give yourself little rewards when each chunk is completed to keep the motivation going. For example, once you have tracked your expenses, watch an episode of your favourite show.

- **Challenge: Find the why**

   In order to complete a task, we often need to understand why it is important that we do it. What's your clear end goal? For example, if you want to save for a holiday, make a vision board of where you are going and why. Keep this somewhere you can see it as you build up the savings.

SIDEQUEST

Find your own strategies to stay motivated

What are some personal strategies that might work for engaging your interest-based nervous system?

- Think of one chore or task you don't enjoy or that you're always putting off — it can be anything, money-related or not.
- Then in the 'My strategy' box, write how you could engage your interest-based nervous system to help you feel more motivated about this task.

Strategies for staying motivated

MOTIVATION FACTOR: INTEREST
We are stimulated by activities or topics that interest us personally.
My strategy:

MOTIVATION FACTOR: NOVELTY
We are drawn to new experiences and things that pique our curiosity.
My strategy:

MOTIVATION FACTOR: URGENCY
We act under pressure because we are driven by a time limit or a deadline.
My strategy:

MOTIVATION FACTOR: CHALLENGE
We rise to a challenge that has a defined goal, an end point and especially a reward.
My strategy:

Hopefully you are getting a good picture of why money management purely being *important* is not going to charge our brain into action. However, receiving an overdue bill with some red on the paper (yep, don't worry: I know what they look like because I've received them too) can spring us into action.

Why? Let's look at this through the lens of motivation factors: the overdue bill has created *urgency*. Sometimes it is even a *challenge* if we don't immediately have the cash flow for the bill. So now our brain might be motivated to respond and pay the bill.

Money management

Money management and **financial literacy** is not something that naturally comes easy to humans, neurodivergent or not. But add in a feeling of shame around our finances and money — for things like for getting into debt, spending too much or not sticking to a budget — and financial literacy becomes increasingly harder.

It's not something we were taught in school. And unless you had financially literate parents or caregivers, money is often not something that is spoken about in home settings either. Much of the financial advice and guidance out there is great. However, it is given with a neurotypical lens. You may have read and heard things like:

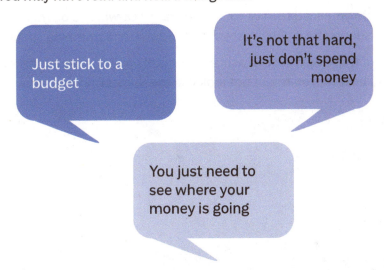

Just stick to a budget

It's not that hard, just don't spend money

You just need to see where your money is going

Understanding ADHD and Money

What this well-meaning advice misses, though, is that it fails to take into account ADHDer's executive functioning challenges, financial trauma and emotional dysregulation. Some neurodivergent people might also have another area of neurodiversity such as dyscalculia (which is like a financial dyslexia).

This book is intended to do what I call '*take the typical advice and sprinkle it with some neurospice*'. Not all money management advice is something we need to throw in the bin. A lot of it is very sound and can get you far in your financial journey. However, we need it to make sense for our brains, our mental capacity and our current skill set.

> ## SIDEQUEST
>
> ### Sprinkle it with spice
>
> We can flip the typical advice, sprinkle it with some neurospice and make it work for us.
>
> - Do you need a budget? Or would it be better for you to manage your cash flow?
> - Do you really need a fancy spreadsheet? Or are you actually better off using a pen and a notebook?
> - Do you need to save for a 'rainy day'? Or will you be more successful if you're motivated to save for something specific?
>
> Each of these options can achieve the same result. It's just that what works best for you might not look like the 'typical' advice.

ADHD and money

The ADHDers I have worked with and spoken to often feel that typical financial advice can make them feel overwhelmed or unsure of where to start. If they're unable to save, people can feel ashamed, like they have failed. Similarly, ADHDers who spend more money than they'd like can feel guilty about it.

It's easy to educate people about money and finance, but it's quite another thing to understand the ins and outs of a neurodivergent brain when it comes to managing money.

Executive functioning, or the struggle to be 'practical'

Typically, financial management takes executive functioning to succeed.

What do we mean by 'executive functioning'? For a neurotypical brain, the brain's command centre helps it to manage functions relating to organisation and time management. But for the ADHD brain, these executive functions aren't so straightforward.

Executive functioning can include:

- planning (like budgeting)
- prioritising (say, you need money for rent rather than the latest tech you've been eyeing off)
- impulse control (you see something you instantly 'need', and you get it without thinking twice)
- self-monitoring (e.g. tracking your spending)
- focus (like staying committed to your goals and saving).

Straight off the bat, it seems like we are doomed. (We're not — but more on that later.)

How we might struggle with executive functioning

Executive function	ADHD challenge	Typical result
Planning	Can be difficult to think ahead or stick to a plan.	Missing bills, accruing fees, feeling stressed and guilty.
Prioritising	Can be driven by interest rather than 'importance'.	Spending money on impulse purchases without stopping to think.
Impulse control	Find it hard to resist unplanned spending and overspending.	Running out of money for necessities or getting into debt.
Self-monitoring	Not easy to stay on track with spending and bills.	Feeling lost, dreading checking your bank balance, running out of cash.
Focus	Can be tricky to keep tasks consistently top of mind.	Abandoned savings goals.

How Money Makes You Feel

Successful financial management also assumes we don't feel things like shame and guilt around our finances. And it would be remiss of me to not say that even neurotypical brains can carry around some shame or guilt when it comes to money.

There are a lot of different opinions out there when it comes to what we 'should' do with our money. Whether we're neurodivergent or neurotypical, we can judge ourselves — and others —harshly if it seems like we're not living up to that idea of 'should'.

Many people feel pressured to keep up with friends or family when it comes to lifestyle spending. And it's probably safe to say that most people have made an impulse buy that they regretted later.

Financial management also assumes that we haven't been through some financial trauma in our lives. Sometimes our past difficulties can make it even harder to get a handle on the present. How we feel about those past experiences can have a real impact on how we spend and save in the present. For example, if someone has experienced financial instability, scarcity or loss in the past, they might feel compelled to avoid looking at bills or their bank balance. They might spend more money as a way of soothing negative emotions like stress. Or they might go the opposite way and hoard their savings, scared to spend on 'unnecessary' purchases or experiences.

So what's different for emotions related to money when it comes to ADHD? People with neurodivergent brains can feel emotions much stronger. We struggle with emotional regulation, so when we feel guilty for overspending, for example, it can be harder for us to overcome that feeling and move on. We can carry the feeling with us, and use this instance as evidence that we will stuff up down the track.

We can also struggle with naming the emotion we are feeling, which makes it difficult for us to process that feeling and move through it.

How money makes you feel is a complex issue! We'll explore more on how to identify your emotions around money in the next chapter.

This is where *ADHD Money* comes in

This book is designed to share information and tips with the ADHD brain in mind so you can find your own financial empowerment.
You can learn how to prioritise, curb and/or plan for your impulse purchases. With the right strategies, you can focus on what you want for your financial future, rather than what society or someone else tells you to want.

You get to look at finances with a different lens.

My goal is to help you find what works for you. And this book will be with you every step of the way.

With the right strategies, you can focus on what *you* want for your financial future, rather than what someone else tells you to want.

CHALLENGE
Money and me

You can use the worksheet as the starting point of your financial journey.

Think about the following 'Money and me' questions, then write down your answers.

1. What do you like about money? Does it bring you security? Do you like that you can buy things? Do you enjoy earning it?

2. What *don't* you like about money? Does it make you feel stressed? Do you struggle to keep money in your bank account? Do you want to earn more?

3. What are you good at with money? Are you good at checking your bank account? Are you great at cancelling subscriptions you don't use? Are you good at budgeting?

4. What are you maybe *not* so good at with money? Do you not enjoy budgeting? Do you struggle to check your bank account? Do you have trouble remembering to check in with your financial goals — or to set goals in the first place? Whatever it is, you won't be the only one who feels this way.

It's OK to be honest in this challenge; there are no right or wrong answers. This activity is for you to understand your thoughts and feelings about money. Recognising those thoughts and feelings now will help you as you move through this book.

I've filled out an example that might help you get started. Part of me wanted to use examples I've seen and heard from speaking to people I've worked with in the past. But I want to help you be vulnerable and if I want this book to truly help you, I need you to know where I have come from. Where my mindset *was* compared to where it is now. And I need you to be comfortable with writing down what is truly in your mind and heart, rather than just the surface stuff.

Your responses may be completely different to mine; your money story may be more positive, or more negative, and that is completely fine. Be truthful; no-one will see this, unless you decide to share it with them.

Your thoughts are valid, too. If the only thing you like about money is to earn it, write it down. If you think that spending is the only thing you are good at when it comes to your finances, write that down too.

This activity is not about shaming you for how you feel or act around money. Let me say again: *anything that feels true to you is valid*.

Money and me worksheet

1. WHAT I LIKE ABOUT MONEY

I like that money has afforded me a house for my family to live in, to buy the food I want to eat and to keep my family safe and well.

I also like that it buys me things. While I am not overly materialistic, I want to be able to afford most of the things I want without having to stress about it. I like to have plenty of money, as growing up we didn't have much.

2. WHAT I DON'T LIKE ABOUT MONEY

I don't like that money makes me feel like a bad person for wanting it. It can also be hard to manage with a partner that has a completely different way of managing finances.

I don't like that I feel bad for not being typical with my money. Money has made me feel a lot of shame and guilt and has taken away from the good things that money can bring.

3. WHAT I AM GOOD AT WITH MONEY

I am very good at spending money! I am also good at being able to plan what I want to do with money. I am good at keeping track of what is coming in and out of my bank account (cash flow). I am now good at thinking more positively about money, because I have done a lot of work on my money mindset.

4. WHAT I AM NOT SO GOOD AT WITH MONEY

I am not great with saving money, but I am getting better. Sticking to a budget is hard. Trying to manage finances with a partner who does things differently is hard too.

Money and me worksheet

1. WHAT I LIKE ABOUT MONEY

2. WHAT I DON'T LIKE ABOUT MONEY

3. WHAT I AM GOOD AT WITH MONEY

4. WHAT I AM NOT SO GOOD AT WITH MONEY

CHAPTER 2
Navigating Emotions and Money

In this chapter we get into ...

- Why strong emotions affect money management
- How your go-to strategies for self-regulation can help
- How to identify your money emotions more precisely
- Emotional spending, including:
  - Overspending
  - Impulsive spending
  - Social spending
- How to identify your spending habits — and curb them

Big mood

Emotions. We all have them, feel them and have to learn how to manage them.

But did you know that neurodivergent folk tend to feel emotions far more intensely than a neurotypical person? Say an unenthusiastic hello to **emotional dysregulation**. This term refers to a difficulty in managing and controlling emotional responses.

Emotional dysregulation can involve intense, prolonged and/or inappropriate emotional reactions in everyday situations. The power of that emotional response also makes it harder to return to a 'baseline' emotional state — that is, a more neutral state where we don't feel this emotional stress.

While your emotional responses may not be part of the ADHD diagnostic criteria, professionals acknowledge that emotional dysregulation plays a core part of how we experience ADHD.

Emotional dysregulation can show up in many different forms. It's not unusual to feel:

- irritable
- angry
- easily excited
- impulsive
- frustrated
- anxious
- sensitive to criticism.

And those feelings might manifest in:

- outbursts of anger
- mood swings
- struggling to make decisions
- taking risks
- crying easily (and then not being able to stop crying once you feel a bit better … anyone else?)

These emotions and behaviours are often seen by others as impulsive emotional outbursts.

I remember when I was 10, I had a friend call me 'moody' and they said they didn't want to hang around with me anymore. At the time I didn't know I had ADHD and it caught me so off guard that I have never forgotten it. I also didn't understand how I was being moody. In my view, I was just being me. Looking back, this was part of my long and confusing journey with my emotions.

Tips to self-regulate

You may already be familiar with some strategies you can use for *self-regulation*. There are lots of different activities ADHDers can use more generally to help us process our emotions, stay focused and keep on track. It can take a while to figure out what works best for you.

This gets into a much bigger topic than tackling your finances but it's good to be aware that if you've developed strategies to help you self-regulate more generally, you can call on these strategies *before* you deal with your finances.

So, before you stop to check your bank balance, sit down to track your spending or expenses, or any other money task that might have you feeling stressed or anxious, take the time to use your go-to techniques to regulate yourself.

These techniques might include:

- *physical movement*. Take a quick walk around the block, have a dance to some music you love, do some jumping jacks, play with a fidget toy or bust out your favourite yoga moves.
- *food*. If it's been a while since you've eaten, check in with yourself. It's easy to get distracted when you're hungry.
- *mindfulness*. Try some deep-breathing exercises, a body scan or a short meditation. Apps like Headspace or Calm can help with this.
- *chunking*. Break down your big task into smaller 'chunks'. A series of small tasks can be less daunting, and completing each one feels more rewarding. You might even use a timer or a checklist to stay motivated as you work through each smaller task.
- *rewards*. Give yourself credit when it's due! Positive reinforcement goes a long way. That might mean taking a moment to pat yourself on the back. Or it could be that you set a specific reward, like watching an episode of your favourite show or making a smoothie. (And there's no achievement too small.)

Think about what activities or actions you take to keep cool and calm when you're stressed or feeling dysregulated. Could those same actions help you in mentally preparing to tackle your money?

Acting on a feeling

At this point, you might be asking, 'Why are we talking so much about emotions?' Well, our money is very much tied to our emotions — I believe more than most people realise

And the thing with emotions is that they create actions. Sometimes the emotion might start with a clear thought — but sometimes those thoughts or beliefs might be subconscious. (We'll come back those subconscious thoughts in the next chapter.)

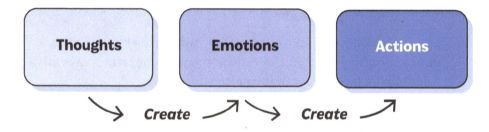

When it comes to what you've been taught about money management, how often has the role of emotions come up?

It seems like money management is always about 'practical' actions like budgeting, cash flow, saving ... not so much about *how not to dip into your savings when you're feeling tired and want to buy the whole grocery store*.

On the flip side, we know all about 'retail therapy', don't we? In movies and television, it's when a girl (the character is always female, isn't she!) is upset or sad, and her friend will take her out for a shopping spree. Then often they show the character feeling so happy afterwards because the distraction of a good shop has solved all her problems.

So we learn from examples like this that buying things will make us feel better. But does it? Or does it just fuel our thoughts and emotions further? Because now we've gone and spent money that perhaps we didn't want to, on things we don't value, all as a way of trying to manage our emotional state.

More realistically, that character in the movie might wind up feeling guilty for buying things she didn't need or didn't have the money for. But this makes me wonder: how can we use emotions to our *advantage* when it comes to money management?

If our thoughts create emotions, which then create action, then we just need to think more positive thoughts. Easy, right? In theory, yes. But in reality, this can be far more difficult than that, especially for the more intense emotions we feel as ADHDers.

So before we delve into a money mindset that will help shift our *thinking* (that's in chapter 3), let's run through how we can better understand and harness our *feelings* when it comes to money.

How to recognise our emotions — and what to do about them

Identifying and naming our emotions can be hard. For example, anxiety and excitement can feel like similar sensations in the body. In my experience, when it comes to money, the emotions most often discussed are anxiety, shame, guilt, stress, happiness and excitement.

You may be thinking 'Wait, you're an accountant, not a psychologist.' And you're right, so if you want extra help to identify and manage your emotions, working with a professional like a psychologist or counsellor can help immensely. But for now, the Wheel of Emotions (overleaf) is a good resource to have on hand. I often use this wheel to help me speak with clients about their emotions around money.

The wheel consists of:

- primary emotions (the inner circle)
- secondary emotions (the mid circle)
- tertiary emotions (the outer circle).

There might be emotions on the wheel that you have never heard of or used in describing thoughts and feelings. That's totally fine.

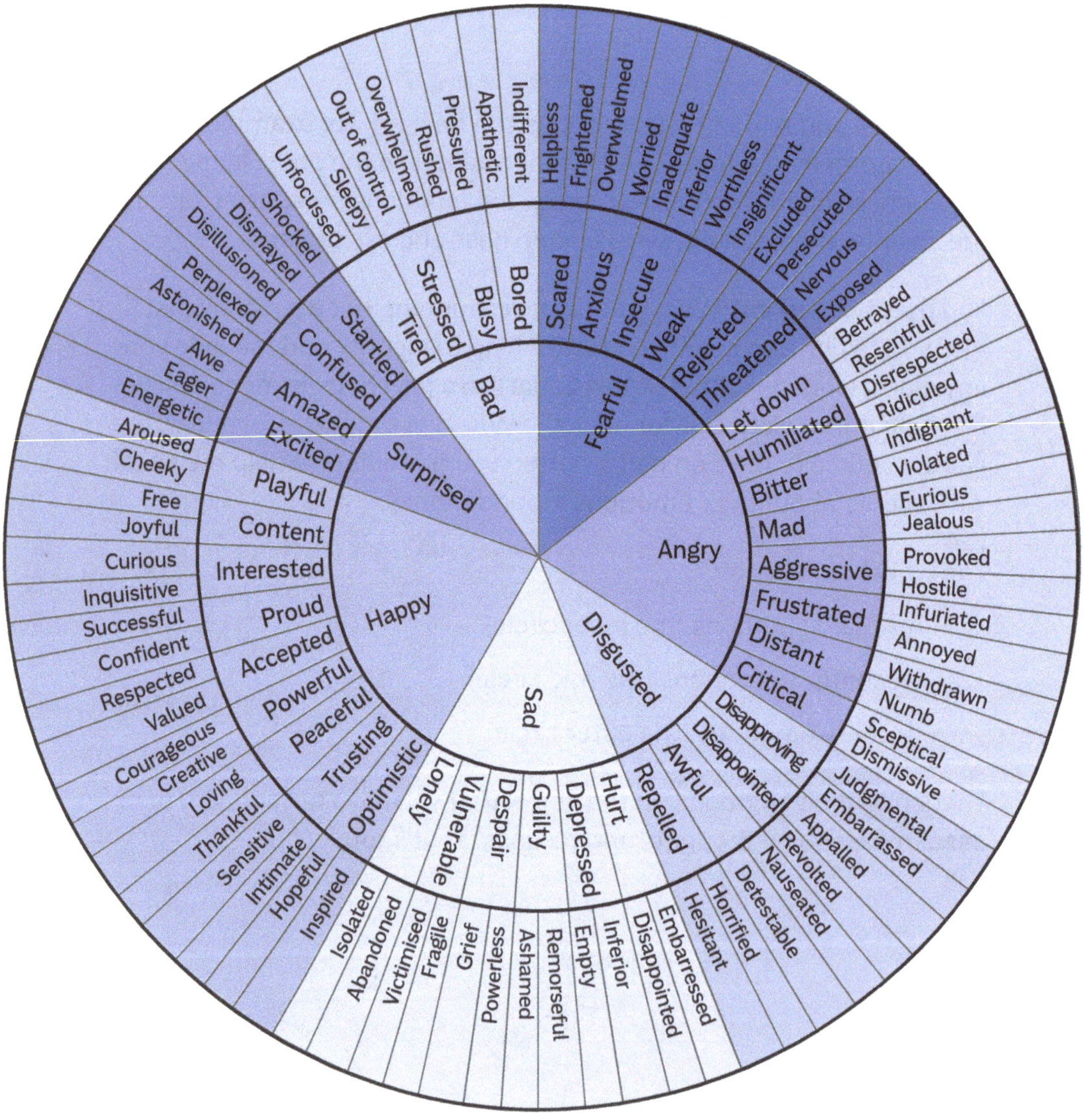

Bad
Bored
Busy
Stressed
Tired
Indifferent
Apathetic
Pressured
Rushed
Overwhelmed
Out of control
Sleepy
Unfocussed
Fearful
Scared
Anxious
Insecure
Weak
Rejected
Threatened
Helpless
Frightened
Overwhelmed
Worried
Inadequate
Inferior
Worthless
Insignificant
Excluded
Persecuted
Nervous
Exposed
Angry
Let down
Humiliated
Bitter
Mad
Aggressive
Frustrated
Distant
Critical
Betrayed
Resentful
Disrespected
Ridiculed
Indignant
Violated
Furious
Jealous
Provoked
Hostile
Infuriated
Annoyed
Withdrawn
Numb
Sceptical
Dismissive
Disgusted
Disapproving
Disappointed
Awful
Repelled
Judgmental
Embarrassed
Appalled
Revolted
Nauseated
Detestable
Horrified
Hesitant
Sad
Hurt
Depressed
Guilty
Despair
Vulnerable
Lonely
Embarrassed
Disappointed
Inferior
Empty
Remorseful
Ashamed
Powerless
Grief
Fragile
Victimised
Abandoned
Isolated
Happy
Optimistic
Trusting
Peaceful
Powerful
Accepted
Proud
Interested
Content
Playful
Inspired
Hopeful
Intimate
Sensitive
Thankful
Loving
Creative
Courageous
Valued
Respected
Confident
Successful
Inquisitive
Curious
Joyful
Free
Cheeky
Surprised
Excited
Amazed
Confused
Startled
Aroused
Energetic
Eager
Awe
Astonished
Perplexed
Disillusioned
Dismayed
Shocked

SIDEQUEST

Exploring the Wheel of Emotions

How can you use this wheel to find and identify your emotions more clearly?

1. Think of money. For example, think of sitting down to create a budget or review your spending from last week.
2. Now, think about how you feel. Look at the options in the inner circle at the very centre of the wheel. Which of these primary emotions do you feel most strongly?
3. Look at the secondary emotions next to your primary emotion — those in the middle circle of the wheel. These are the different ways that the primary feeling you've identified can be felt and understood. From this next level of feelings, can you identify which option resonates the most with you?
4. Next, you can work further outward to the third circle, the tertiary emotions. This outer circle helps you pinpoint the dominant emotion you are feeling even more precisely.

Let's say you feel fearful. This is one of the primary emotions, and it can serve as a starting point for further exploration.

But fearful is a big emotion! There are many reasons you might feel fearful and many different ways you might feel it. So if you stop at fearful, or another primary emotion in the inner circle, then it's hard to see and understand the underlying reason you might feel this way. That means it's also hard to put together a plan to help you work through that emotion — and conquer it when it comes to your finances.

(continued)

So you will find it useful to get more specific. If you make your way outward from fearful, you might think about the options on the wheel and realise your fear is because you are feeling anxious about the task ahead.

And if you keep moving outwards to the tertiary emotions, you might be able to see that you are *really* feeling more overwhelmed than worried.

This is where you can start to help yourself through what you are feeling. Because at this point you can go 'I am feeling overwhelmed about looking at my spending. How can I make this a less overwhelming task for me?'

An action plan to help combat that feeling of overwhelm might be to:

- Break down the activities involved. Smaller steps can feel less intimidating and create a more frequent sense of reward as you check off each step. You might even create novelty by doing each step in a different place or a different way.

- Set a 15-minute timer to help you get started and create a sense of urgency.

- Visualise an end point. A clear goal helps create a sense of challenge. It also helps to make the goal feel more real, which can increase your interest.

CHALLENGE
The thoughts and emotions worksheet

Now it's your turn to give it a go.

You can use this worksheet to explore your own money feelings. But first, I've shared an example that's already filled out.

Note: emotions can be heavy; it's OK if you are unsure about the secondary and tertiary emotions. Even starting at the first (inner) circle will help you to identify the thoughts and emotions you are having. That's still a perfect first dive into this activity.

You may not be sure about your next steps yet. But we'll cover lots of tips and strategies in the coming chapters so you might come back and fill in the last two boxes when you see a good idea for how you're feeling.

Remember: we are not here to shame ourselves for not completing a task on the first go. You can always come back to it later.

Thoughts and emotions worksheet

I AM THINKING THAT...

I don't want to create a budget because I know I won't stick to it.

PRIMARY EMOTION	SECONDARY EMOTION	TERTIARY EMOTION
Sad	Guilty	Ashamed

HOW COULD I MAKE THIS TASK LESS OVERWHELMING?

I can try a smaller, more targeted budget.

I can budget just for food over the next week.

This will help me track my cash flow for one week, as well as give me a taste of creating a budget in the future.

THE NEXT STEPS ARE ...

1. Track how much I am spending on food for the next 7 days.

2. Each day, I will check in with how I am feeling about my money.

3. At the end of 7 days, I can review where I spent my money. This will give me a sense of when and why I buy different foods (e.g., a big grocery shop for cooking meals, small top-ups for missing items throughout the week, takeaways when I am tired or need a reward).

4. By tracking how I spend for one week, I can get an idea of what I might need to budget for food every week – and where my food spending makes me happiest.

5. Read chapter 3 about mindset.

Thoughts and emotions worksheet

I AM THINKING THAT ...

PRIMARY EMOTION	SECONDARY EMOTION	TERTIARY EMOTION

HOW COULD I MAKE THIS TASK LESS OVERWHELMING?

THE NEXT STEPS ARE ...

Emotional spending

Our thoughts create our emotions, which create our actions.

Think about the last time you overspent. Do you remember what you were feeling?

- Were you excited to be out of the house?
- Were you exhausted from work or because you were scrolling your phone late at night?
- Were you feeling like you had to buy your colleague a going-away present?

When I talk about emotional spending, I'm talking situations such as overspending, impulsive spending and social spending.

Emotional spending differs from regular spending in that emotional spending occurs when we let our emotions drive our money decisions.

Three kinds of emotional spending

$	Overspending	Spending way more than you budgeted
🕐	Impulsive spending	Spending as soon as you see something without taking the time to think about it
♥	Social spending	Buying out of obligation, guilt or maybe even excitement, such as for a gift or expected contribution. (This can be a combination of overspending and impulsive spending.)

Overspending

Overspending can be money you spend on things for yourself or for others. The spending might be on impulse or related to an event you hadn't planned for. It might even be for an emergency that you can't avoid. Or it might be for something you had expected but you get carried away and spend more than you'd planned to.

Overspending will happen. It's what you do *after* it happens that will help or hinder the success of your financial management.

Not helpful when you've overspent: spiralling deeper into overspending because you figure you have blown your budget anyway now.

So what *is* helpful?

What to do when you overspend

Action	Why is this helpful?	Result
Acknowledge that you have spent too much.	You'll confront the issue head on.	By recognising and admitting to yourself that you overspent, you can face up to the situation and think of next steps (rather than avoid the problem).
Have self-compassion.	You'll feel better about the situation, which will make it easier to move forward.	Self-compassion helps to prevent feeling bad about yourself — like feeling shame or getting stuck on the idea that you messed up. This makes it easier to take positive actions with your next steps.
Remember that one action doesn't define you.	You'll recognise that this doesn't make you a bad person or 'bad with money'.	A positive view of yourself will help you see a mistake as an opportunity to learn and grow.

This positive mindset shift is something that will take practice. Even I struggle to stay positive sometimes. It's all too easy to slip back into a negative mindset or speak negatively to yourself.

But persistent practice is something that will help you make that positive mindset more of a habit. Remember the little peptalk I gave in the Introduction? *Being persistent* is key.

Impulsive Spending

Pretty much everyone spends impulsively — us neurodivergent humans just tend to do it more often. From shopping online or in person, whether it's something big or small, it is simply money that you spend without really thinking it through.

If it happens from time to time, it's not a big deal. But when impulsive spending happens often, it can cause financial stress. I caution ADHDers against vowing *never* to impulsively spend; it's in our neurotype, after all. However, I firmly believe we can *decrease* how often we spend impulsively.

How to tackle impulse spending

1. *Awareness is key.* Acknowledge that you are impulsively spending. This can come with its own fair amount of shame and guilt, so expect to feel these emotions.
2. *Understand the emotional drivers at the time of the spending.* How were you feeling? What was happening in your life at the time?
3. *Implement some tools to help you.* We will go through these shortly.

It's important to mention that while tools and strategies are great help, you also need to get to the *cause* of the impulsive spending. That could involve something like therapy or coaching.

Tools and strategies might be duct tape if used on their own — meaning, they will just cover up what is really happening. But if used in conjunction with getting to the underlying cause of your spending, tools and strategies can be powerful.

In the past when I frequently shopped impulsively, it was because I was unfulfilled in my life. Not all aspects of my life. Just some of them. I was in jobs that didn't suit me, I had no idea how to slow down my fast brain and I was dealing with a lot of anxiety from undiagnosed ADHD. This led me to shop to make myself feel better, which worked in the short term but in the longer term led to dissatisfaction and, of course, financial disaster.

CHALLENGE
Identify why you're spending

Let's start with some self-awareness.

On the following worksheet, you can start to collate why and when you are spending. That means you'll start to get a picture of what triggers your emotional spending.

1. Set a timeframe to track your spending. This might be seven days or two weeks.
2. During that time write down:
   1. anything that you impulsively purchased
   2. anything that you overspent on.
3. Include:
   1. the date
   2. the thing you spent money on
   3. where or how you bought it (e.g. online, the supermarket, walking home from work, late at night).
4. In the 'Why' column, write down any of the three kinds of spending we identified earlier: overspending, impulsive spending or social spending. You might find it is more than one.
5. Finally, in the 'Feeling' column, write how you felt at the time, physically and emotionally. The Wheel of Feelings can help you with this.

Once you can see what motivates your emotional spending, you can start to acknowledge those causes — and then use strategies to manage your spending more intentionally. (Again, therapy or coaching can really help with this too.)

Emotional spending tracker

DATE	PURCHASE	WHERE/HOW	FEELING
1 August	Clothes	Online, late at night	Tired
2 August	Chocolate bar	7/11	Hangry
4 August	Streaming subscription	Online, looking for a movie	Bored, tired
5 August	Coffee and cookie	Morning, on my way to work	Wanted a pick-me-up
7 August	Birthday gift for Tom	Online, evening	Anxious, stressed
10 August	Lunch	Work lunch break	Frustrated, hungry
10 August	2 x books	Online, lunch break	Frustrated, tired
11 August	Groceries	Changed my mind about dinner and stopped to pick up something different on way home	Hungry
13 August	Clothes	Online, late at night	Excited about an up-coming social event; guilty for splurging

EXAMPLE

Emotional spending tracker

DATE	PURCHASE	WHERE/HOW	FEELING

Emotional spending tracker

DATE	PURCHASE	WHERE/HOW	FEELING

Social Spending

As I mentioned earlier, social spending can overlap with both overspending and impulsive spending. With this kind of emotional spending, you might find yourself spending money out of obligation, guilt or even excitement.

Some scenarios where you might feel forced to spend even if it isn't practical include:

- A colleague is leaving the workplace, and you feel obligated to buy them something or contribute to a leaving gift.
- It's a loved one's birthday, and you find yourself spending more than you planned to get them something they'll like.
- You agreed to go out for dinner with friends, but you would prefer to save that money.
- Your friend has started a crowdfunding campaign for their band, and you feel guilty when you see them sharing it on social media every day.
- Work is having a Secret Santa, and you have to buy a present to contribute.
- Your BFF is having a hens/stags weekend away in another city, and you feel like you have to go even though flights are too expensive.

This is a bit of a controversial topic, so if you disagree with it, that's OK. But many of these scenarios are born out of social construct, such as the going-away gift for the colleague. Is buying a gift a kind thing to do? Absolutely. But does that mean you have to take from your rent money to do so? No.

You might feel embarrassed that you can't afford to chip in or buy a gift, and in that case, there are workarounds! For example:

- You can offer to catch up with the colleague when you are in a better financial position for lunch.
- If you are crafty or handy, you can make something.
- You can purchase a gift that you *can* afford at the time, if the cost of the joint gift is too much.

The point here is that a situation like giving a gift or spending time with loved ones doesn't have to break the bank. You can think outside the box and the social construct and instead do what feels good for you *and* your finances.

Self-compassion helps to prevent feeling bad about yourself. And that makes it easier to take positive actions with your next steps.

How to curb emotional and impulsive spending

We've covered the different kinds of emotional spending and some of the things that might motivate us to spend in this way. Now it's time to chat about some tools and strategies you can implement.

As I said before, these tools and strategies are really useful for recognising and changing your spending behaviours. But to create a lasting change, you need to couple these tools with working on your emotions and your mindset.

And again, you will note that I use realistic language around money and spending. I never talk about *stopping* impulsive spending as this is unrealistic. Trying to completely and totally stop a behaviour that is innate to our neurotype can set us up for feeling more guilt and shame. That's why it's so important to have self-awareness *and* self-compassion.

So let's get into it!

The 24-hour rule

This is essentially putting time in between you and the purchase. It's a way to delay gratification, without feeling like it.

You tell yourself that if you still want the item in 24 hours, then you can go get it. You can play with the timeframe if 24 hours seems too long. You might do 12 hours to start off with. Once it becomes second nature, you can also extend the time. Sometimes I'll use seven days or until the next pay day.

I can tell you, in most cases, you will forget you even wanted the item. But, if you do still want it, you can check to ensure it's within budget and cash flow — and maybe even in line with your values too.

Take a picture or write a note

When one of my children wants something at the shop that just isn't in the budget or that I don't want to spend money on, I tell them we can take a picture of it so we can keep it in mind.

In the past I always just said no, and debating would ensue. When I started saying I would take a photo of it for down the track, maybe for their birthday or Christmas, the change was interesting. There was no more debating (well, maybe a little) and far less stress for me.

This plays into a strategy of not telling yourself no as well into the 24-hour rule. You know how when you tell yourself *no*, it's all you can think about? Same thing here.

If you say no, you can end up thinking about that item nonstop, until you give in and go purchase it. Whereas if you take a picture of it, you are telling yourself that you're not saying no, but you aren't getting it *right now*, and you have a record of it in case you decide to get it later. But again, more often than not, you will forget about the item after the initial burst of interest.

Speak with someone you trust

Having someone you trust to talk to about potential purchases can be helpful. It can give you an objective conversation about what you *really* want to spend money on.

Sometimes we can't really think clearly about what we want to spend money on. We might buy kitchen items when we already have one, or even multiple, of the same thing. We might want to buy clothes that don't go with what we already have (which, therefore, means we need to buy even more clothes to go with the new thing). We might buy a gadget that we can't use, just because it looks cool or someone else has it.

At these times, it can be hard to think logically. We can let our emotions decide for us. So it helps to have another person you can discuss these things with.

A word of caution here: the idea is *not* that the trusted person *controls* what you spend your money on and how much. They are merely a sounding board so *you* can decide what you do.

Have an impulse-spending bank account — and budget for it

Like I said before, it's not practical to think you'll *never* spend impulsively. So one strategy is to set yourself an amount you *can* spend on impulse, and put that amount in a different bank account. The separate account should have its own bank card, separate from your other money.

Once the impulse account is empty, it's game over. Of course, you can replenish it each time you get paid, so remind yourself of that.

Setting aside money you're 'allowed' to spend impulsively can also help you feel less guilty about spending money mindlessly.

Cheat sheet: Four strategies to slow your spending

Strategy		Explanation	Why it works
🕐	The 24-hour rule	Tell yourself to wait 24 hours before making a purchase.	You avoid giving yourself a hard no by telling yourself that if you really want it, you can still have it later. (Often, you'll forget all about thing you wanted. And if not, you have time to check your budget or cash flow before you buy it.)
📷	Take a picture or write a note	Take a photo or note of the item for your wish list instead.	You'll feel reassured that you have a record of the thing you want, so you won't forget about it. (But again, once you file it away, you'll find you can happily forget about it when the impulse fades.)

Strategy	Explanation	Why it works
Speak with someone you trust	Discuss potential purchases with a trusted person for an objective view.	Bouncing your ideas off a third party can help you think logically about whether you really need or want that thing.
Have a dedicated impulse-spending bank account	Set aside a specific amount for impulse buys in a separate account.	Give yourself permission for guilt-free impulse spending — with a limited budget.

CHALLENGE
Emotional spending worksheet

The last activity in this chapter is the emotional spending worksheet.

In this chapter you've had some time to think about the relationship between emotions and actions, as well as your own emotional spending habits. This worksheet can now help you journal about your personal thoughts and emotions around money more generally.

That isn't always easy to do. It can be hard to put some of the things we think and feel into words, especially if those things are negative. But remember, there are no right or wrong answers here. This is just a space for you to explore your relationship with money, so you can find what does — and doesn't — work for you.

And if you have some big realisations as part of this process, again, remember that a counsellor or therapist could help you work through this process too.

Use the method that works best for you

Remember: you can also use your favourite journal or notepad to do these activities, if you prefer to use something you feel more comfortable with.

If you struggle to write, then speak. You might record voice memos on your phone or just go through the activity out loud. You might even talk through it with someone you trust. Often, expressing yourself verbally can help you work through your thoughts more clearly.

Emotional spending

ONE THOUGHT I HAVE ABOUT MY RELATIONSHIP WITH MONEY IS ...

I am not good with money, and I can't learn to manage it. I fear that I will never get to a point where I am comfortable with my finances.

WHERE DOES THIS THOUGHT COME FROM?

I was never taught about money or finance, and I'm unsure where to start. My ADHD traits play a role in this.

WHAT EMOTION DOES THIS THOUGHT CREATE?

I feel ashamed that I struggle to 'adult' with money in the way society expects me to.

WHAT ACTION OR INACTION DOES THIS THOUGHT RESULT IT?

This thinking is stopping me from looking at my spending and creating a budget that suits me. It holds me back from trying new things.

WHAT CAN I DO TO SELF-REGULATE AND CREATE NEW THOUGHTS?

Before I deal with money, I can go for a walk first, to calm my nervous system. Then, once I feel more regulated, I can get curious and think about what things I can tell myself instead of the thoughts above.

For example: I can take just one little step towards learning about money. With each small step, I will get more and more comfortable.

Emotional spending

ONE THOUGHT I HAVE ABOUT MY RELATIONSHIP WITH MONEY IS ...

WHERE DOES THIS THOUGHT COME FROM?

WHAT EMOTION DOES THIS THOUGHT CREATE?

WHAT ACTION OR INACTION DOES THIS THOUGHT RESULT IT?

WHAT CAN I DO TO SELF-REGULATE AND CREATE NEW THOUGHTS?

CHAPTER 3

Reframing Your Money Mindset

In this chapter we get into ...

- Your personal money story
- The money mindset you currently have
- How to embrace a positive mindset for better money outcomes
- The financial values that shape your actions
- What financial success looks like *for you*

Mindset matters

Before you skip this part because you think mindset is a big bunch of fluff, I urge you to keep reading. Even if you skim read this chapter, I'm confident you will pick up something new.

A lot of people don't realise they have a certain way of thinking about money. A lot of our thinking is subconscious — bubbling away in the background.

But the way we *think* about money (our mindset and our beliefs) has an impact on our daily financial decisions and the way we *feel* about money.

Did you know that our mindset is created when we are really young? By seven years old, we have learned our money habits and mindset. This can be hard to shift once we start becoming responsible for our own money as an adult.

The good news is that your money mindset does not need to be fixed. You can create new money beliefs and a positive money mindset thanks to 'neuroplasticity', a concept we will get into a bit later in this chapter.

Creating a positive mindset around money is imperative to your financial success.

A negative mindset can leave you feeling disempowered and demotivated. A positive money mindset will get you through the tough times when it comes to money management. This mindset will ensure you don't throw in the towel.

Throughout this chapter we will look at how your money mindset and values shape your actions.

One thing it's important to remember when we talk about money mindset for ADHDers is that success for us may look different from success for neurotypical people. However, we can achieve our goals with money without following the 'normal' rules or typical ways of getting things done.

I have listened to so many experts and interacted with many an ADHD coach, and they all echo a similar sentiment: once you understand how your brain, nervous system, and past experiences works with ADHD, you can begin to live life more authentically.

This is what I envisioned for you reading this book and doing the activities. To understand and uncover exactly what you want to do with your money by filtering out society and anyone else who tries to tell you that you are doing it wrong.

For now, let's start with your 'money story'.

Uncovering your money story

Everyone has a money story. If you don't know yours, this is exactly what I'm going to help you uncover.

Your money story starts from when you were probably only a few years old. Even at that age, you would have started to take in ideas and habits around finances, even if you weren't aware of it.

If your family struggled with money, your young mind might have taken in situations like the stress around getting to pay day with enough money for food, unpaid bills piling up or maybe even the utilities getting cut off.

If your upbringing was more affluent, perhaps you felt the excitement of being able to afford a huge annual holiday with your family or expecting toys throughout the year. You might have started to notice that earning lots of money involved hard work and sacrificing time with family.

Or perhaps you were somewhere in between. Maybe there was enough food and you had warm showers, but holidays were for the rich and toys were only for Christmas.

As already mentioned, research suggests that our key beliefs and values are fixed by seven years old, before we even have the chance to choose for ourselves or be aware of them. This is why the way we think about money is so ingrained in our subconscious. That can make it difficult to change *if* we aren't aware of *how to change it*.

A positive money mindset will get you through the tough times when it comes to money management.

CHALLENGE
Identify your money story

Answer the questions in this worksheet to write out your money story. I've filled out an example for you.

Identifying your money story will help you see the underlying thoughts and beliefs that influence your emotions and your actions when it comes to money management.

And once you can see those thoughts and beliefs clearly, you can think about whether they're helping or hindering you with your money and spending today.

That's the first step in changing your money mindset: knowing what works for you and what you need to change.

My money story

MY EARLIEST MEMORIES OF MONEY ARE ...

Seeing my mother stress about money. There was talk about money being low and my mother having to work really hard for only a little bit of it. There wasn't much family talk about money; it was more overhearing what my mother would say. This made me think that money was a taboo topic and should not be spoken about.

I remember that if we did have a bit of extra money, it would be spent on a bit of extra-nice food or something like that. We didn't have any savings or have anything more than the very basics.

HOW DO I REMEMBER FEELING ABOUT MONEY AT A YOUNG AGE?

I didn't like money. Once I was old enough to know that some families had money and others didn't, it made me jealous of kids that had more money than me, the ones who could afford to go on holidays or get the latest tech or toys.

I remember being around 10 years old and knowing that one day I wanted to be rich so I could afford to do things and buy whatever I wanted.

HOW DID MY PARENTS, CARERS AND OTHER ADULTS IN MY LIFE REACT TO MONEY?

I remember most of it being negative. There would be stress when we'd be running low on money (which was most of the time) but happiness if, for some reason, we had a bit more money than usual.

I also remember my parents would comment about 'rich people' and that things like nice clothes or nice cars were only for rich people, which we were not.

Money was the sole source of stress or happiness.

WHAT ARE SOME WAYS I THINK THIS MIGHT HAVE IMPACTED HOW I FEEL ABOUT MONEY NOW?

This is probably why I avoided money management as I entered adulthood. I was never taught how to think about money or how to manage it. I thought of money as good or bad, rather than a resource.

Money can still sometimes govern how I feel about myself.

One thing my mother taught me, which I still think about to this day, is to make sure your bills are always paid on time — and to pay them before anything else!

My money story

MY EARLIEST MEMORIES OF MONEY ARE ...

HOW DO I REMEMBER FEELING ABOUT MONEY AT A YOUNG AGE?

HOW DID MY PARENTS, CARERS AND OTHER ADULTS IN MY LIFE REACT TO MONEY?

WHAT ARE SOME WAYS I THINK THIS MIGHT HAVE IMPACTED HOW I FEEL ABOUT MONEY NOW?

Your money beliefs

Now that you have an understanding of your money story, let's tackle money *beliefs*.

Our money beliefs often come from our childhood as well. Think of them as a result of our money story:

- how our parents or other significant adults spoke about money to us
- how they spoke about money around us
- how they expressed their opinions about money
- whether we had lots of it or very little.

These are the kinds of things that shape our mindset around money, and we bring that influence into our adulthood.

For example, if your parents worked really hard but had little money, you may believe that money is hard to come by or that you also need to work really hard to bring in money. This may make you feel ashamed for spending money and that you should be holding onto it.

On the flip side perhaps the mindset that evolved from your money story instead encourages you to seek out easier ways of earning money. You might welcome a new age of earning money so you don't go through the stress and hardship that your parents did.

Do you have a fixed or growth mindset when it comes to money?

Whether you have a *fixed mindset* or *growth mindset* will indicate how successfully you can change your money beliefs.

These terms were coined by psychologist Carol Dweck, and they describe ways that we think about ourselves and our abilities.

SIDEQUEST

A fixed mindset versus a growth mindset

Here are some of the more general ways that a fixed versus growth mindset might shape our beliefs and actions.

Are there any particular points in the following table that resonate strongly with you?

Fixed mindset	Growth mindset
Abilities and skills are something you're born with and don't change.	Abilities and skills can be developed if you make an effort to learn and practise.
Challenges are something to avoid because you are likely to fail.	Challenges are opportunities to grow and improve your skills.
Effort will only get you so far, so putting in too much seems pointless.	Effort is how you make progress and eventually succeed.
Obstacles and setbacks are reasons to give up.	Obstacles and setbacks are opportunities to learn.
Seeing others succeed makes you feel threatened.	Seeing others succeed inspires you and makes you want to aim higher.
Feedback is personal and usually feels like an attack.	Feedback is helpful and shows you how you can progress even further.

Fixed mindset

If you have a fixed mindset, you might believe you are just plain not good at something — like money. And that means you're less likely to try new ways of managing your money. You might believe that budgeting or saving simply doesn't work for you.

But as we've said before: you are *not* 'bad with money'; you just have to find strategies that work with your ADHD brain, rather than against it.

If you have a fixed mindset, you might think things like:

> I can never earn that much money.

> I am not allowed to buy myself nice things.

> I can't go out with friends because I don't have the money.

> I don't know how to budget so I won't even try.

> I would invest if I had better financial literacy.

Growth mindset

On the other hand, if you have a growth mindset, you are more likely to embrace the idea that you can learn and develop new skills over time. And positive outlook about your ability to learn and grow means you are more likely to be persistent and try until you succeed.

If you have a growth mindset, your internal thoughts might be:

> Even if I can't do a full budget, I can budget for groceries

> I wasn't taught financial literacy, so I'm going to learn more about it.

> I can spend in line with my values.

> Going out with friends doesn't have to cost much money, if any at all.

> I wonder if there are ways I can earn more money.

CHALLENGE
Identify your money mindset

It's normal to feel shamed or anxious around finances. But if you stick with a fixed mindset, you will avoid learning about how to build wealth and experience financial wellness.

I hope, because you've picked up this book, you are already open to learning about money. And the good news is, a fixed mindset itself isn't fixed: a growth mindset is something you can practise. We'll come back to this in a bit.

But first, answering the following questions will help you identify your money mindset and beliefs.

My money mindset

HOW DO I FEEL ABOUT MONEY? CIRCLE THE WORDS THAT RESONATE

Anxious	Avoidant	Bored	Optimistic
Excited	Open to learning	Impulsive	Ashamed

WHAT BELIEFS DO I HAVE ABOUT MONEY? CIRCLE YES OR NO

I believe I can't make more money.	Yes	No
I believe I need to completely stop spending.	Yes	No
I believe I can learn about money.	Yes	No
I believe I can create financial wellness to suit me.	Yes	No

DO I HAVE A FIXED OR GROWTH MINDSET?

If you circled mainly words like 'anxious' and 'avoidant' in the first box and 'Yes' to the first two questions in the second box, you are more likely to have a fixed money mindset.

If you circled mainly words like 'optimistic' and 'open to learning' in the first box, and 'Yes' to the second two questions in the second box, you are more likely to have a growth mindset around money.

HOW IS MY MINDSET IMPACTING MY FINANCIAL SITUATION?

....
....
....
....
....

The power of positive thinking

I know, I know, 'positive thinking' can sound a bit mumbo jumbo. But studies have shown that positive thinking really can help you with your mental and physical health. And if positive thinking can help to do something as amazing as extend your lifespan then, yes, you can harness that power to deal with money.

So let's chat quickly about how a positive and negative mindset might affect your thoughts, emotions and actions when it comes to money specifically.

Positive vs negative money mindset

Positive mindset	Negative mindset
You are more open to learning new things about money.	You're stuck in the old way of managing your money, even if it doesn't work.
You make proactive choices to manage your bank account, like automating payments and savings.	You are more likely to not look at your bank account in fear of what you have spent.
You are more likely to accept help with your finances.	You are ashamed that you need help and don't feel worthy of it.
You can tackle financial setbacks with persistence and resilience.	You are more likely to avoid financial challenges and decisions.
You are optimistic that you can create wealth.	You are more likely to keep living pay to pay because it's what feels comfortable to you.
You embrace the idea of earning more money.	You are less likely to seek out promotions or higher paying jobs, or building revenue in your business.
You feel good about spending money on what truly matters to you.	You stress about spending too much or on the wrong things.

Change your mindset

So if our mindset is fixed, or negatively skewed, what can we do about it?

Change our mindset! Easy, huh?

Well, yes and no.

The theory is simple: our brains are made to be able to change. This is what we call 'neuroplasticity', and it refers to the brain's amazing ability to change, learn and even reorganise itself in response to stimuli and experiences.

Our brains can create new neural pathways — that is, new connections between the parts that send and receive signals. These changes to the brain can even be physical. Neuroplasticity helps us to absorb and analyse new information and adapt to different environments and situations.

Our brains are most flexible in childhood, but we keep this incredible capacity to learn and change throughout our lives. Yep, even our ADHD brains!

So all we have to do is create new:

- neural pathways
- habits
- belief systems.

OK, in practice, it's a little bit harder than that. Rewiring your brain like this will take *persistence*. But it is possible.

SIDEQUEST

Your brain's neuroplasticity — beyond money

We're focusing on mindset and money in this book. But there are other strategies that can support your brain's ability to learn and grow.

You might have heard this advice before when it comes to ADHD, in terms of tools you can use to boost focus, mood and executive functioning. Mindfulness techniques, physical exercise and even ADHD medications can work to maximise our brain's incredible ability to learn, grow and rewire itself.

Our brains are made to be able to change. Yep, even our ADHD brains!

CHALLENGE
Change your money beliefs

But let's get back to the money stuff. I want to introduce you to my five-step process to help you through some unhelpful beliefs you might have around money.

This process will help you identify where your beliefs have come from and analyse if they are true for you or not.

Let's walk through each part of the process.

1. Where did this thought come from?

   Did it come from your parents, friends, social media? Have a think if you can pinpoint where you have picked this belief up from.

2. Is the thought 100% true? Why or why not?

   Once you start writing down why you think this belief is true or not, you will start to uncover unconscious thought patterns or limiting beliefs you may not know you even had!

3. List the evidence you have that it isn't true.

   Do you consciously know better than what this belief is trying to tell you?

4. If a friend tells you they have this belief, what would you say to them?

   If you wouldn't talk to a friend how you talk to yourself, then you are likely saying things to yourself that are negative or untrue.

5. What thought can you replace the unhelpful thought with?

   Find a more helpful belief that you can replace the unhelpful one with.

Now, make your way through the next worksheet. As usual, I've given you an example to start you off.

Reframing Your Money Mindset

My money beliefs

MY THOUGHT OR BELIEF ABOUT MONEY

I will never be able to earn as much money as I want.

WHERE DID THIS THOUGHT COME FROM?

This is from my childhood and knowing that we were not rich people. There was a clear divide between those who had money and those who didn't, like us. It was instilled in me that I had to work really hard for only a bit of money.

IS THIS THOUGHT 100% TRUE? WHY OR WHY NOT?

No, it's not. I know I can earn as much as I want to if I break through the barriers that I face.

THE EVIDENCE I HAVE THAT THIS BELIEF ISN'T TRUE IS ...

There are so many successful people out there who are neurodivergent and earn lots of money.

IF A FRIEND TOLD ME THEY HAD THIS BELIEF, WHAT WOULD I SAY TO THEM?

What do you think you need to do to break down this limiting belief? Could you see a coach or a therapist? Could you journal about it and ask yourself why you have this belief and what you need to do to break it down?

You 100% have all the skills and knowledge to make your dream a reality!

WHAT THOUGHTS CAN I REPLACE THE UNHELPFUL THOUGHT WITH?

How much I earn doesn't define who I am.

I can be successful in my own way.

There is a future version of me earning the money that I want to earn.

What is one thing I can do today to move me in a forward direction?

My money beliefs

MY THOUGHT OR BELIEF ABOUT MONEY

WHERE DID THIS THOUGHT COME FROM?

IS THIS THOUGHT 100% TRUE? WHY OR WHY NOT?

THE EVIDENCE I HAVE THAT THIS BELIEF ISN'T TRUE IS …

IF A FRIEND TOLD ME THEY HAD THIS BELIEF, WHAT WOULD I SAY TO THEM?

WHAT THOUGHTS CAN I REPLACE THE UNHELPFUL THOUGHT WITH?

CHALLENGE
Find your new beliefs

Now that you've thought through some of the beliefs that aren't working for you, it's time to find some new, more helpful ones.

For this challenge, I invite you to take a look back at the beliefs you wrote down already in the other worksheets in this chapter. If there is a certain belief in those worksheets that you want to change, now is the time to change it.

For each unhelpful belief, write a new statement that takes a more positive, helpful perspective on your relationship to money. I've shared some examples of what this might look like in the next worksheet.

There are lots of different ways you can help your new beliefs take hold. You might start your day by repeating a couple of your most important ones to yourself out loud, as affirmations. You could keep a visual reminder of your new money beliefs somewhere prominent (like on your desk, your fridge or a cork board). Or if you keep a journal (more on this in chapter 6), you might practice writing your new beliefs in your journal regularly.

These beliefs aren't just fluffy sayings to repeat in the mirror. Choosing a new belief and committing to it in this way aims to help your brain etch in new neural pathways. That means you are helping your brain get on board without even having to think about it. By using the process above in 'my money beliefs' worksheet, you can start to change how you think about yourself and your finances.

Really believing these statements may take a bit of time, but it's worth it. As I always say, being *persistent over consistent* is key.

Here are a few examples of old versus new beliefs to start you off.

Old beliefs vs new beliefs

OLD BELIEF	NEW BELIEF
I should be saving more money.	I should save as much as I need to for my own financial goals.
I don't understand money and can't learn about it.	I don't need to know everything but can learn what I need to know.
A smart watch or a smart home is a waste of money.	Tools and tech can make it easier for me to set reminders, which helps me stay organised and on schedule.
I should clean my house more often.	It's OK to hire a professional if I need my time and energy to focus on other things.
I believe that spending money on prepackaged vegetables is bad.	Prepackaged vegetables make it easier for me to make healthy food.

Old beliefs vs new beliefs

OLD BELIEF	NEW BELIEF

Personal story time

I've had to do *a lot* of mindset work around money. I grew up with a single mother who took time off work to care for me (and my siblings) and, when I was old enough, she went back to work. She didn't earn a lot of money so we were either on government payments or minimum wage.

My money story (in a nutshell) was that money was hard to come by. Nice things and holidays were only for rich people. And if we did come into money, it was only for bills and food. There was very little left over for anything else. Takeaways were a very special treat and only once in a while.

This money story created beliefs for me such as: money is really hard to come by, and if I want to earn good money, I have to go to university and get a corporate job.

I found it impossible to save because I never learned financial literacy. When I had spare money, it was spent on whatever I could find because I didn't even feel comfortable holding on to it.

I had to shift my internal beliefs about:

- what money meant to me
- what wealth meant for me
- what I actually wanted my beliefs around money to be, instead of believing what others believed.

It was hard work but a completely worthwhile task to change my beliefs in this way. It has helped me achieve things I never thought possible.

It doesn't happen all at once. To this day, I am still uncovering new beliefs that do not serve my financial future. But I can quickly identify those beliefs now, and then change them up, thanks to the activities I am sharing with you in this book.

Redefining what financial success means

By now, I hope you are figuring out that you get to decide what *financial success* and *financial wellness* mean for *you*. It's so easy to get caught up in someone else's idea of what it means to be financially successful. Everyone has something to say about another person's financial situation.

Most of us have been on the receiving end of comments like:

> Why are you spending money on that?

> Shouldn't you be saving more money?

> Why don't you put more money on your mortgage?

> Why are you buying prepackaged vegetables when you can just buy whole ones and cut them up yourself?

In situations like these, you need to remember that not everyone has ADHD. Not everyone knows your true financial position and not many people are qualified to give you financial advice.

You get to decide what *financial success* and *financial wellness* mean for *you*.

CHALLENGE
Visualise your success

With that mind, I invite you to finish this chapter with something really fun. I want you imagine that you have the best possible financial life.

This is a powerful visualisation exercise that is going to help you understand where you want to be. It's also the first step in thinking about your money values and priorities (something we'll get into more in the next chapter).

What does financial success look like to you?

- How much money are you earning?
- What kind of job do you have?
- Where are you going for your groceries?
- What does your savings account look like (choose a target number)?
- What are you doing on your weekends?
- Are you going on an annual holiday? Where to?

You get the idea. Now, write down your answers on the next worksheet.

Don't hold back. No-one will see this except for you.

Visualise your success

CHAPTER 4

Managing Your Expenses

In this chapter we get into...

- Why expenses can feel so overwhelming
- The importance of cash flow
- The benefits of tracking your expenses
- Some strategies that can make tracking your expenses easier
- An expense audit (i.e. figuring out where your money goes)
- Your money values
- Your financial priorities
- Whether your values and priorities align with your spending

Taking charge of your money

Managing expenses can be a challenging task for anyone. But for individuals with ADHD, it can be particularly challenging. From impulse purchases and difficulty with planning to challenges in keeping track of bills and budgeting, the everyday financial responsibilities can often feel overwhelming.

As we explored in chapter 2, impulsivity can lead to unplanned spending. Beyond our thoughts and emotions around unplanned spending, there are practical consequences: this kind of spending can result in overlooked bills, missed due dates and extra fees and charges.

When I work with other ADHDers and their finances, a big area of stress is expenses. Tracking their expenses, looking at what they've spent and even looking in their banking app can be things they put off until the stress builds and builds.

This chapter is all about helping you feel more confident in looking at your expenses — which then allows you to be more confident in keeping on top of them.

Expenses

If the word 'expenses' brings up some emotions or feelings in your body, then you aren't alone. Expenses are one of the most talked-about things when it comes to your money.

Something you might have heard before is to simply 'decrease your expenses' to improve your financial health. But in reality, it's not always that simple!

Add to that the way other people judge our money choices, and it can make expenses feel overwhelming. We're constantly being told what to spend our money on, with experts and people we know telling us that things we like to spend our money on are frivolous.

Sometimes we don't even know what we need to spend our money on, because there are so many demands and surprises to juggle.

All this can make us want to avoid thinking about our expenses at all. But I'm here to help expenses become less scary for you. In this chapter, we will figure out where your priorities lie when it comes to spending.

The first step is to get comfortable at looking at *what* and *where* you are spending.

Cash flow

We will chat more about cash flow in the next chapter, but here we'll start with a brief overview.

You may have heard the saying 'cash is king'. When people say this, they're not talking about physical cash but about *cash flow* — the way money comes in and goes out.

There's a good reason that cash flow is important in a business. A high percentage of businesses fold within the first two to five years because of cash-flow issues. It's not the budget or the forecast that causes issues. It's a lack of cash-flow management. Problems with cash flow will crumble a business faster than many other factors.

Personal finances aren't much different. Run out of cash, and you run out of the ability to buy food and keep a roof over your head. Or you go into debt. Which then creates further cash-flow issues, because now you need to pay off that debt. Which creates *more* stress.

This is why it's so important to know what your expenses are. That knowledge is not about shaming yourself into spending less. It's to help you evaluate whether your spending is in line with your lifestyle and values, so you can prioritise what you can afford.

Tracking your expenses

When I work with ADHDers and their money, most of them come to me not knowing how much money they need to cover their expenses or what they are spending on more generally. Having a look at their expenses is often the first thing we do together to get a good picture of their financial health.

For example, when was the last time you looked at your subscriptions? We often forget that we've signed up for something like a streaming service, and we can continue to pay for that subscription for months (or even years) before we notice they're still taking our money.

Why tracking your expenses matters

What are some of the benefits of tracking your expenses?

- *Awareness*. Being aware of your spending habits is powerful. 'Out of sight, out of mind' is real. Tracking your spending will help you keep your money management front of mind.

- *Knowledge*. Knowing where your money needs to go (and where it actually goes) will empower you to make informed decisions about when and how much to spend. You'll have a more confident understanding of how to use your money.

- *Reduced anxiety*. The more you do a task, the less anxiety you tend to feel around it. Regularly tracking your expenses normalises this activity, making it less daunting and less stressful.

Strategies for tracking your expenses

In the following table, you'll find a range of strategies that can help you track your expenses:

- Make it simple
- Audit your expenses
- Limit your time
- Habit stack it
- Use visual aids
- Body doubling

If you remember the ADHD motivation factors from chapter 1, you'll notice the following strategies use some of these same factors to keep your interest-based nervous system engaged.

Cheat sheet: Strategies for tracking your expenses

Make it simple	The most effective method is often the simplest. When we try to make something too complicated, we can get overwhelmed and start to avoid the task.
	Motivation factors: **Challenge:** Keeping your tracking simple allows you to focus on the end goal.
	Tips: If money spreadsheets and apps are complicated and overwhelming, go back to basics: try writing out your expenses with pen and paper.
Audit your expenses	Review your spending from the past month. Once you see where you spend, you can assess where your spending is serving your best interests.
	Motivation factors: **Challenge:** This activity has a clear, defined goal for you to achieve.
	Tips: Bring some **novelty** by using your favourite pens, pencils and highlighters and make it more fun.
Limit your time	A task can seem more overwhelming if there's no end in sight. Nobody wants to spend all day on tracking their spending – but you can do it for just 5, 10, or 20 minutes.
	Motivation factors: **Urgency:** Setting a time limit can boost your sense of urgency and thus help you stay on task.
	Tips: Increase the **challenge** by giving yourself a reward if you complete the activity on time. Boost the **urgency** by setting a timer for 5, 10, or 20 minutes when you try the audit worksheet.

(continued)

Habit stack it	**Habit stacking** is a technique that has worked for a lot of my clients. Popularised by James Clear in his book *Atomic Habits*, habit stacking involves pairing your expense tracking with a habit you already hold and enjoy. Something like this will help you look forward to the activity and make expense tracking more bearable.
	Motivation factors: 🎧 **Interest:** This strategy pairs expense tracking with another activity you already enjoy.
	Tips: Example: if you have a nighttime drink (like a cup of tea or Milo®) before bed, you can sit down with that and your expense tracker and track that day's or week's expenses. Similarly, one of my clients would go weekly to a café, grab a drink and something to eat and do their expense tracking there. Think about a daily or weekly habit you enjoy that you could stack this way. You might even bring some ✨ **novelty** by trying a few different habits.
Use visual aids	If you opt for a paper-based system, using highlighters, colourful pens, templates and so on can help your brain stay more engaged. If you opt for a digital system, you might like to use charts and graphs to make tracking more engaging.
	Motivation factors: ✨ **Novelty:** Bringing colour to your tracking method can keep it feeling fresh and interesting and bring a layer of fun.
	Tips: If the first system or method you try doesn't work for you, don't be afraid to try another one next time.

Body doubling	**Body doubling** is a strategy where you pair with another person while you work on a task. You can do this with a friend or family member or even use an app like Focusmate to body double you while you do your tracking. When we see someone else working, it becomes easier for us to mirror their focus and productivity. Body doubling can be really affective for the ADHD community as we are more likely to do the thing when we are doing it alongside someone else.
	Motivation factors: 🎧 **Interest:** A social connection can help you to feel more supported and engaged, rather than feeling isolated or anxious. ⛰ **Challenge:** Having another person present can increase our sense of accountability and even create a positive sense of peer pressure. (You want to work as well as they do.)
	Tips: The key to keeping you on task is that you: - both have something to do - minimise talking - set a time limit (e.g. 30 minutes) - both confirm what the steps are ahead of time. Setting a time limit will also engage your sense of ⏰ **urgency** and ⛰ **challenge**.

Managing Your Expenses

Finally, you might like to engage a financial coach, financial consultant or an ADHD coach to help you create a system to track your expenses. A coach or consultant can help you with the different steps to organise your finances as well. You can also work with them to tailor your expense tracking strategies in a way that engages the motivation factors that work best for you.

Expense audit activity

If you are yet to start tracking your expenses, the audit in the following challenge will help you. I'd encourage you to do an expense audit regularly. But even if you start by just doing this task once, it will help you determine where your expenses are at.

If the word 'audit' makes your skin crawl, reframe it! Call it something else. Perhaps, 'Goodness me, where has my money gone?' or 'I am curious about what is in my account'. Say this to yourself without shame, without any expectations and with compassion for yourself.

Essentially, you want to investigate what is in your bank account. What subscriptions you have, where you are spending your money and how much you are spending.

Now, I know this can cause anxiety in many ADHDers, to the point that we avoid it. I want you to go into this without judgement. What is in your bank account doesn't mean anything about you personally.

It's a good idea to have some self-regulation tools on hand. For example, you might want to grab a weighted blanked or soft toy, fidget tools or your favourite drink. Or you might pop on some music you like or a show you like to watch (that you've watched a million times before, so you don't have to concentrate on it).

Even if you prefer to use apps or a spreadsheet, this activity is one way you can do audit *right now*.

What's in your bank account doesn't mean anything about you personally.

CHALLENGE
Do a quick audit of your expenses

Here is what you need to do:

1. Regulate yourself in your favourite way *before you start this challenge*. Take a quick walk around the block, have a quick dance to music, get something to eat if it's been a while since you've eaten. You get the idea!
2. Grab your favourite pen or a pencil.
3. Bring up your transactions for the past month, in either your banking app or via the bank's website. If a month seems too daunting, just start with the past week.
4. List each expense and the amount. *Don't fill out the last column yet*.

Once you've done steps 1–4 you're ready to move on to the second part of the activity.

You can use this tracker to identify where you'd like to cut back on spending. We'll use subscriptions as an example of how to do this.

1. Use the last column to run through the tracker and identify all the expenses that are subscriptions. Next decide if you want to keep each subscription. Put a Y next to the ones you will keep and an N next to the ones you want to cancel.
2. Grab a highlighter, pen or pencil, and highlight or circle the subscriptions you want to cancel.

Go through with the plan

If you can act now, then do it. For example, if there are any subscriptions you want to cancel through your phone app store, then grab your phone now and cancel them straight away. It will take less time than you think.

Otherwise, set a date/time you will make the change. Use a strategy like body doubling if you need help getting started.

Expense tracker

Month:

Date	Description of expense	Amount	Keep? Y/ N

Expense tracker

Month:

Date	Description of expense	Amount	Keep? Y/ N

What to do with this information

It's great to have the data, but it's even better when you know what to do with it. You will want to take this tracker with you into chapter 5, to use for budgeting and/or your cash flow.

Meanwhile, some final advice on expense tracking: try not to fall into the trap of being perfect with your tracking. Often we don't do something because, for example, we don't have the right tools or we can't find the pen we want to use. We can feel analysis paralysis where we have trouble deciding what the 'best' method or strategy is — for example, whether we want to use paper or digital tools.

Doing something is better than doing nothing. The stars don't need to be aligned for you to look at your expenses.

And remember the golden rule: *persistent over consistent*!

If you don't want to track your expenses every day, that's OK. If you don't track your expenses for a few days or weeks and feel you have 'fallen off the wagon', then just pick up where you left off.

You will be in a much better position even doing a little bit every now and then, rather than not doing it at all. And the more you do it, the more comfortable you will be with it.

> ## SIDEQUEST
>
> ### Check in with yourself: How are you feeling?
>
> If you feel some shame or guilt during or after your expense audit, then you might try revisiting the challenges in chapter 3 to help you explore those money emotions. As I've said before (and will probably say again): it can also help to reach out to someone like a coach or therapist who can help you work through these feelings.

Try not to fall into the trap of being perfect. Doing something is better than doing nothing.

Let's talk money values

If you've never considered what your **money values** are, or you have no idea what I'm even talking about, you're in the right place.

What many people don't realise is that our money and our **personal values** are interconnected in a profound way. By understanding your core values and aligning your financial choices with them, you can create a more purposeful relationship with your money, and it can even help you curb impulsive spending!

On the next page are some values to get you started, but the list can go on! Although it's not that you *should* have a hundred and one values. Pick as many as you want to, but don't let it get overwhelming (otherwise you will find it hard to translate values to action).

Your personal values could be

👪	Family
🕊	Freedom
🏠	Security
🌱	Personal development
🎁	Giving to others
🎓	Education

How do you choose your values?

You will find that your money values are very closely tied to your personal values. For example, if you personally value time spent with your children, you might find you're more likely to value spending time and money to take them to the movies or other fun adventures. If you value education, you might find you are more likely to spend money on courses or personal development.

You can also ask yourself:

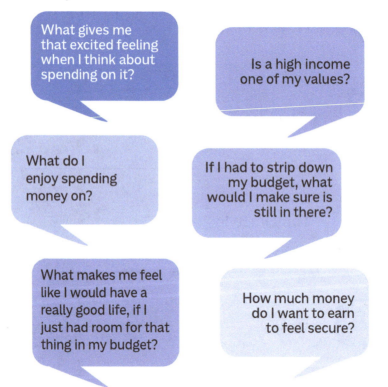

The thing about values is that they can change throughout our lives. What you valued as a 20-year-old is probably vastly different to what you might value as a 45-year-old. So, if it helps you decide what matters most, remember, your values are not necessarily forever; some might be but many will change.

It is really important to note here that your money values are yours and yours alone. Not everyone is going to agree with them. That's OK. They don't need to. Only *you* need to be on board with your values.

CHALLENGE
Find your money values

This activity follows the steps we've just talked through:

1. **List your personal values.**

    These are the things that matter most to you in life. You might get some ideas for this from the personal values list on p112. Or you might have your own ideas and values to add.

2. **Answer the worksheet questions.**

    This will help you explore your money values.

3. **Compare your personal values to your money values.**

    Is your current spending in line with what you value most?

My money values

WHAT ARE MY PERSONAL VALUES? WHAT MATTERS MOST TO ME?

Financial stability, health, freedom, knowledge, security

WHAT DO I ENJOY SPENDING MY MONEY ON? WHAT MAKES ME FEEL EXCITED TO PURCHASE IT?

Family holidays, nice food, education, clothing or household items that will last

WHAT IS ESSENTIAL TO KEEP MONEY FOR IN MY BUDGET?

Good food, kids schooling, family outings, mortgage, basic utilities, streaming services, pet items and care

HOW MUCH MONEY DO I NEED TO EARN TO FEEL SECURE?

Income of $100 000 (or a combined household income of $150 000 if you have a partner.

WHAT ARE MY MONEY VALUES? DO THEY ALIGN WITH MY PERSONAL VALUES?

My money values align with my personal values:

1. *I like to spend money on good food, so that aligns to my health value.*
2. *I like to earn money by working for myself, so I have the freedom to do what I want and need, and the freedom to do things with my family whenever we want to.*
3. *I invest money into education, so that fulfills my knowledge value.*
4. *I like to work in an area I enjoy and that I am good at so I can earn what I need in order to have financial stability and security.*

My money values

WHAT ARE MY PERSONAL VALUES? WHAT MATTERS MOST TO ME?

WHAT DO I ENJOY SPENDING MY MONEY ON? WHAT MAKES ME FEEL EXCITED TO PURCHASE IT?

WHAT IS ESSENTIAL TO KEEP MONEY FOR IN MY BUDGET?

HOW MUCH MONEY DO I NEED TO EARN TO FEEL SECURE?

WHAT ARE MY MONEY VALUES? DO THEY ALIGN WITH MY PERSONAL VALUES?

What are your financial priorities?

Our ADHD brains do not prioritise easily. Unfortunately, it's just one of those ADHD things. Everything is important, all at once, and we struggle to define what needs most attention.

However, once you figure out your money values, you can more easily figure out what your **financial priorities** are.

It's simple. You'll automatically prioritise the things that are further up your value ladder.

For example:

- If you value good food, you will want to prioritise a higher grocery budget.
- If you value mental wellness, you might prioritise coaching or therapy.
- If you value a high income, you might prioritise finding a job based on how much it pays.

Do you see where this is going?

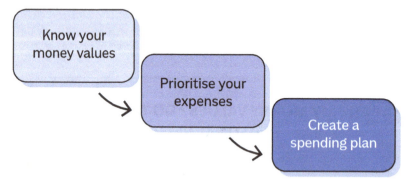

Knowing your money values means you can prioritise your expenses. And that means you can tell your money where it needs to go and create your spending plan!

We're going to tackle that spending plan in the next chapter.

CHAPTER 5
The ADHD Spending Plan

In this chapter we get into ...

- Why budgeting can be hard
- ADHD-friendly budgeting strategies
- How to create your personal spending plan
- How to track your cash flow
- Using a budget template (if you *really* want one)

Introducing the ADHD spending plan

One of the first things I did when I started ADHD Money is create the ADHD Spending Plan. This plan is a different way for people with ADHD to budget.

Budgeting when you have ADHD is hard. Many people can create a budget, but then they find it hard to stick to it. There can be a few different reasons people generally don't stick to a budget:

- It's too restrictive.
- The budget doesn't align with their current lifestyle.
- The format is too confusing.
- They don't *want* to stick to the budget.

Essentially, the simplest method is often the best method.

The ADHD Spending Plan involves two stages:

1. creating your ADHD-friendly budget
2. cash-flow tracking.

I find a budget is brilliant to get an understanding of what is coming in and going out of your bank account, and it's a very easy way to see whether you have money left after accounting for all your expenses.

Now, I'd like to point out that I have a love–hate relationship with budgeting. My accountant brain loves it; I can easily see if I have a surplus or deficit of money and where I am spending more money than I expected. My ADHD brain, however, can get frustrated with budgeting.

I can get caught up asking myself, 'What expenses do I put where?' and worrying there are expenses I have forgotten to put in. In other words — perfectionism making an appearance.

The beauty of the ADHD Spending Plan is that you can do either step (budgeting or tracking) first, *and* you can do just the one step, or both. It's customisable. It's flexible. It's exactly what we need for our neurotype.

ADHD-friendly budgeting

When you look for help budgeting, you're likely to find a lot of the same advice. Things like: figure out your after-tax income, write down your expenses, adjust your budget if it needs to change and set realistic goals.

You might get other recommendations, such as tracking your progress or using different budgeting methods (e.g. 50/30/20 budgeting, zero-based budgeting, the envelope system — don't worry if you've never heard of these).

What is kind-of-but-not-really interesting is that most of this advice does not take into account different neurotypes or consider that the reader might have **dyscalculia** (difficulty processing and calculating numbers). Now, I did say 'kind-of-but-not-really interesting' because neurodivergent people are a minority in society. So it's fair to say that 'general' advice won't cover every single person's situation. However, I also think it's fair to say that even if someone might be neurotypical, money can still be confusing and hard to figure out.

For many ADHDers to be successful with budgeting, even more information and more detailed breakdowns are needed. For example, much of the typical finance information around expenses is just 'need' versus 'wants', or determining your 'necessary' versus 'discretionary' expenses. That might be fine for a neurotypical brain, which can distinguish easily between these terms, or for a typical person who might have less emphasis on health and medical spending. But it doesn't work so well for us.

The other issue with just lumping expenses into two categories like 'necessary' versus 'discretionary' is that it makes it harder to see where you can cut out spending if you need to.

Take the cost of living, for example. When the cost of groceries goes up, logic tells us that we might need to cut down our spending in another area to accommodate a bigger grocery budget. But if all our other expenses are just marked as 'discretionary', an ADHDer might go into paralysis analysis, stuck trying to figure out which expenses to remove or cut down on.

Similarly, if we are only marking expenses as 'needs' or 'wants', what happens when we need to cut back on expenses? Where do we start? Which 'wants' should we cut before others?

I decided to develop a system where we can more easily separate our expenses. And it has the bonus of helping you prioritise expenses too!

CHALLENGE
Create your own ADHD Spending Plan

With the ADHD Spending Plan, we're going to break down your money into some more useful categories. With this next worksheet, you're going to look at the following.

Income

How much money do you get each week/month, and where does it come from? This amount should be net of tax — that is, the amount that actually lands in your bank account. List your different sources of income, for example: different jobs, business income, income from shares or investments, income from rental properties, and so on.

Note: this is for people who have tax taken out before their pay lands in their bank account. If you are self-employed, then it might be best to work with your accountant to estimate what this might be.

Tier 1: Necessary expenses

What are the expenses you absolutely *need* to pay? These are the expenses you need just to exist in your day-to-day life, such as rent or mortgage payments, utilities and food.

Tier 2: Valued expenses

What are the expenses you *value* above other expenses? These expenses are not the ones you need to exist but you value these expenses even if you had to find money in your budget for them. This is personal, and you might want to revisit the money values you identified in the last chapter.

Tier 3: Nice-to-have expenses

What are the expenses that might be nice if you had extra money left over? These are the expenses you value the least.

A few notes:

- The answers here are personal. Some of these expenses will be valued highly by one person but only nice-to-haves for another. Some of my tier-2 items might be your tier 1 or tier 3. There is no right or wrong here. Forget what you know about 'discretionary expenses'. This is about *your* priorities.

- Be true to yourself. If you think that something is a tier 1 or tier 2 expense, then no-one gets to tell you otherwise.

- If you are struggling to split your expenses into tiers, don't force it. Take some time to think about what you value most. You can revisit the exercises in the last chapter, and look at your bank account to see where you are spending your money and how you feel spending it.

I've given you an example of how to fill out the sheet, but first I'll explain two personal examples.

For me, one tier 2 expense is Spotify. I *love* Spotify. This is often seen as a want or a discretionary expense, one that should be cut back on if needed. But to me, this is a tier 2 (valued) expense. I use it every single day. Music regulates me, and I like that I can just look up nearly any song I want, in any given moment, and play. That is truly important to me. Spotify can increase their monthly fee (and they have many times since I started using it), but I will still find a way to fit it into my monthly spend. For someone else, this might be a tier 3 expense. However, I get to choose where I spend my money — and I don't have to feel guilty or be shamed into changing this.

On the other hand, a tier 3 expense for me is books. I know for a lot of people this might fall into tier 2. However, at my current stage of life, I just don't value buying books as much as I value some other things.

But if I have some spare money, and I have some books on my wish list, then I will purchase them.

Now, armed with this information, I invite you to prioritise your own expenses.

Need some help?

Some tips for getting through the worksheet:

- Try body doubling — either with an app like Focusmate or a friend.
- Engage with this activity when you have the mental capacity — when you are well rested and have met your basic needs rather than after a stressful day, for example.
- Pair the activity with your favourite food or drink, or tackle it immediately after doing an activity you enjoy.

Your personal spending plan

LIST ALL YOUR INCOME STREAMS
Where does your money come from?

Employment income, business income, income from shares

TIER 1: NECESSARY EXPENSES
Expenses that you absolutely need to pay

Mortgage, medical and medication, groceries, utilities, insurance (car, house, health, etc), phone/internet, personal care, car expenses, school fees, necessary clothing, mental health, expenses related to any of your income

TIER 2: VALUED EXPENSES
Expenses you value above others

Streaming services, music and concerts, clothes for fashion and fun, registrations, books, impulse, spending money, Christmas savings, birthday presents

TIER 3: NICE-TO-HAVE EXPENSES
Expenses that might be nice to have if you have extra money

Holidays, outings (such as the museum, zoo, movies etc.), restaurants/cafes

Your personal spending plan

LIST ALL YOUR INCOME STREAMS
Where does your money come from?

TIER 1: NECESSARY EXPENSES
Expenses that you absolutely need to pay

TIER 2: VALUED EXPENSES
Expenses you value above others

TIER 3: NICE-TO-HAVE EXPENSES
Expenses that might be nice to have if you have extra money

Cash-flow tracking

Whether or not you are planning on making a budget, I highly suggest you look at tracking your cash flow.

Cash flow is the movement of money in and out of your bank accounts. You may have heard about this concept for businesses, but it is an essential part of personal finance as well. Run out of money and you are in jeopardy of not being able to cover your expenses and pay for your essentials.

I recommend managing your cash flow over creating a budget.

A budget is great, but without cash flow monitoring and regular checking of your budget, it's not really of any benefit. A budget is telling your money what to do. But cash-flow tracking is what your money is *actually* doing.

Why tracking can be helpful

The main benefit of cash-flow tracking is that you get real-time data. You can see straight away if you are spending too much or if you have a surplus of money for an emergency or fun spending. Tracking can:

- give you a real-time view of your money
- help you catch potential issues *before* they become problems
- help you spot patterns in your spending (e.g. when and why you tend to spend more money)
- give you an opportunity to adjust your spending to ensure you have enough funds for essential spending.

But more than this, tracking can help you gain a sense of control and, in the long term, help improve your relationship with money. It creates predictability in an area of your money management that might usually feel chaotic.

CHALLENGE
Track your cash flow

Essentially, tracking your cash flow involves seeing what comes in and out of your bank account each day, week or month. (Or, you know, a mix of all three, because we are the poster children for inconsistency.)

If you are new to tracking or find you have lots of little transactions to track, this can become a bit daunting. One hack is to track certain categories. For example, you might start off by tracking only your groceries and food spending. That way, you will get a taste of cash flow tracking, without the overwhelm.

Here are some categories you might choose to track, when it comes to where your money goes:

- income — money from your job, investments, tax returns or anywhere else
- home — rent, mortgage, utilities, home maintenance
- food — groceries, takeaways, eating out
- leisure and hobbies — streaming subscriptions, books, movies, social activities, sports gear
- pet care — food, vet visits, toys
- shopping — clothing, make-up and hair products, gifts, miscellaneous, impulse spending
- transport — public transport, car insurance, petrol, parking, rideshare services
- wellbeing — GP visits, prescriptions, specialists, therapy, physio, wellbeing apps

These are just a few ideas. You might have other ways you think about your income and expenses — or you might have different hobbies, interests and activities to include. As always, use what works for you.

Remember: Be persistent over consistent

Trying to force consistency or shaming yourself over being inconsistent will make you run the other way. Persistence is more important than being perfect. So get out your notebook or spreadsheet when you remember, when your reminder app tells you to, when you have the spoons or when you have set aside time in your calendar.

Cash flow tracker

Month: March

Date	Category	Description	Amount
1 March	Food	Weekly groceries	-$249.50
2 March	Income	Work pay	+$1,250
2 March	Utilities	Electricity bill	-$189.87
3 March	Transport	Weekly transport monthly pass	-$53.00
3 March	Food	Lunch at work	-$17.99
4 March	Food	Quick shop (forgotten ingredients)	-$21.95
5 March	Leisure	Spotify subscription	-$13.99
5 March	Utilities	Internet bill	-$89.99
6 March	Shopping	Clothing	-$55.99
7 March	Leisure	Movie ticket with friends	-$31.00
7 March	Rent	Rent	-$1,450
8 March	Food	Takeaway coffee	-$7.50
8 March	Transport	Weekly transport monthly pass	-$53.00

Cash flow tracker

Month:

Date	Category	Description	Amount

Persistence is more important than being perfect ... You can be inconsistent and still be successful!

If you *really* want to create a budget

Budgets have their place! I have a yearly budget for both personal finance and business finance. However, they kind of just sit in the background while I focus on cash flow. I revisit my budget every now and then to see if anything has changed, and I definitely check in with it at least once a year.

So, if you'd like to create your budget, these are the steps:

1. Review your ADHD Spending Plan and/or expense tracker from last month.

2. Use the numbers there to fill out the budget planner shared here. Estimate one month of your income, expenses, debts and savings.

   - *Income*. Identify the money that's coming in (e.g. from work, investments, interest from savings).

   - *Bills*. Write down your bills due that month (e.g. rent, utilities, car registration, phone and internet).

   - *Expenses*. This box is for your other necessary spending, the stuff you need to pay for beyond the obvious bills. Estimate things such as groceries, streaming services, fuel/gas and school fees.

   - *Debt payments*. Note down your outstanding debts (e.g. car loan, personal loan, mortgage, HECS payment, credit card, AfterPay, ZipPay).

   - *Savings*. Are you going to put any amounts away for your emergency fund, house deposit, holiday fund and so on?

3. Allocate any 'leftover' money.

   - *Extra savings*. Once you've estimated your expenses and debts, do you have anything left over from your income? This is where you can aim to grow your savings. If you have 'extra' money, putting even $5 into an emergency fund is better than nothing! Don't let our 'all or nothing' trait stop you from even putting a small amount of money away.

   - *Your impulse-spending fund*. An impulse-spending fund can be one of your savings accounts as well. It's important to let ourselves be impulsive with money now and then (to the extent we can afford it). A dedicated impulse account means we won't just pull money from other things like our rent or mortgage repayments. We want to be financially stable ADHDers!

A few notes:

- You can also do this budget on a yearly level as well as a monthly level.
- You could pop these same things into a spreadsheet to make it easier.
- If you are feeling that tightness in your stomach because you don't know what decision to make, you can always switch it up down the track.

Remember: you won't make the wrong decision just by *starting*.

Budget planner

Month:

Income	Amount

Bills	Amount

To savings	Amount

Expenses	Amount

Debt payments	Amount

Summary	Amount

CHAPTER 6
Tools and Strategies to Keep the Novelty Alive

In this chapter we get into …

- ADHD and the problem with boredom
- Tools and strategies to keep motivated, including:
  - Body doubling
  - Support groups
  - Journalling
  - Gamifying
  - Coaching and consulting
  - Therapy
  - Habit stacking
- A financial toolbox — ideas for boosting your money management

Keeping things new and shiny

You've probably heard of 'shiny object syndrome'. It's often referred to in the ADHD community for when we get motivated by, but also distracted by, something new and shiny.

Finding a new way to manage your money can often lead to feelings of motivation because it's new, exciting and might give you a feeling that this is *the* thing that is going to save your financial life.

I'm getting excited with full-body tingles just thinking about it! Hello **dopamine**! What is dopamine, you ask? It's a chemical messenger (a.k.a. a **neurotransmitter**) that sends signals in the brain and body. Known as the 'feel good' hormone, it contributes to how people experience pleasure and reward. Because of this, dopamine helps to manage mood and attention.

But for those of us with ADHD, dopamine can come fast and furious — and depart the same way. Which means that when we go full-speed ahead, we can crash and burn rather quickly. We get all that delicious dopamine and the reward centre of our brain lights up, and then we just... get tired.

You may have heard the saying 'It's a marathon, not a sprint'. Well, this couldn't be more true than when it comes to managing your money. A sprint will only get you so far before you move onto something else exciting, new and shiny. But if you know you are in for a marathon, while it might be harder to actually get started, it will be far more sustainable.

Knowing this ahead of time will put you in a good position to put some tools and strategies in place to keep you on track. This will help you to not feel shame and guilt when things inevitably get a bit boring.

Managing your money is a marathon, not a sprint.

What to do when we get bored of it all

One thing I want you to know is that it's OK to feel a bit bored with your finances at times. Not that you need it, but you have my permission to take a break from looking at your money when it all gets a bit too much.

Numbers are my special interest, and even I would sometimes rather stick a fork in my eye than look at my bank transactions! The key is to know how and when to get back on track.

Let me give you a couple of examples.

Pop quiz: What do you do when you get off track?

Scenario	Options
Scenario 1: You've tracked your money for the last few months but, for whatever reason, you don't track this month.	a. Forget the tracking of your money ever existed. b. Acknowledge the absence but get back on track the next day.
Scenario 2: You've been on track with lowering your impulsive spending but one day you aren't feeling great and you buy everything you've been wanting in 30 minutes.	a. Feel immense guilt and decide you are a terrible person. b. Acknowledge what happened and understand that this means nothing morally and you can move on from this.

If you picked (a) in both scenarios, then you're in luck! This chapter will help you put together your very own toolbox of strategies and activities that you can pull out when you find yourself struggling to get back on track.

If you checked (b), then kudos to you! However, you will still benefit from this toolbox of strategies for those times when perhaps you aren't feeling like an A+ student.

And don't feel bad about whichever option you chose. You are not a robot: *you are human*!

Strategies and tools that can help

The strategies in this chapter tap into our key ADHD motivation factors that we talked about in chapter 1. Remember, the ADHD brain operates with an interest-based nervous system, which means it prioritises tasks that feel engaging, exciting or rewarding in the moment.

So our brain is more likely to want to complete an activity if it incorporates one of four key motivation factors:

- interest
- novelty
- urgency
- challenge.

The following strategies can engage our nervous system in different ways. As you'll see, more than one motivation factor can play into each strategy — and you can combine strategies and factors in different ways to maximise your motivation.

> **SIDEQUEST**
>
> ### Start with self-regulating
>
> With any financial task, take a moment to regulate yourself in your favourite way *before you start*. (And if you need ideas for self-regulating, you can revisit chapter 2, pages 32–33.)
>
> Whether it's grabbing a quick snack, doing 10 push-ups to get yourself pumped or using an app for a quick breathing exercise, take advantage of the actions you know work best for you when it comes to feeling good and motivating yourself.

Strategy: Body doubling

You may have heard the terms body doubling or co-working before. (We also talked about this strategy in relation to tracking your expenses, on page 103.)

Essentially, body doubling is when you and another person (or people!) get together and work through something you need to do. You might get together in person, on video or on a voice call.

There is no limitation to when or how you can use body doubling, either. I've known people who not only work or manage their money with other people, they also do the housework, exercise, do assignments — the options are endless!

You can tee up with another neurodivergent human to get on a Zoom call and smash out some bank account tracking or look at your spending plan. Having someone else to keep us accountable can help get our brains and motivation into gear.

Brain motivation factors

- 🎧 **Interest:** A social connection can help you feel more supported and engaged, rather than feeling isolated or anxious.
- ⛰ **Challenge:** Having another person present can increase our sense of accountability and even a create positive sense of peer pressure.

Tools and Strategies to Keep the Novelty Alive   145

Strategy: Support groups

You can join an existing support group for people with ADHD or create your own focused specifically on money. Support groups can be in person or online, or both. Whatever floats your boat.

There are some incredible online groups (*cough* like the ADHD Money Community on Facebook *cough*). But you can simply grab a friend or two and set a time to have regular get-togethers, share your experiences and just be there for each other.

Support groups can help with motivation and accountability. Or they're great for those times you want to whinge about money (with no judgement).

Brain motivation factors

- **Interest:** Sharing our experiences with others is highly engaging, especially if you're a social person.
- **Novelty:** Hearing other people's perspectives and getting new ideas from them can keep things fresh.

Strategy: Journalling

Don't knock it until you try it! Journalling can be incredible for the ADHD brain.

Let's talk about some potential benefits. With journalling, you can:

- get everything out of your head so you don't ruminate
- reduce stress
- regulate your nervous system
- set and clarify your goals
- boost your mental health
- process your emotions

... and, honestly, so much more!

The beauty is that you can journal however you like. Use a pen (or pencil) and paper, type in a Google Doc on your laptop, incorporate colours, use a journalling app on your phone, make a voice recording — whatever format comes most naturally to you.

It's OK if you don't know what to write when you start. Journalling can be hard at first, but with practice it becomes easier.

I've shared some prompts below. You might find that you ask yourself these questions and your immediate thought is 'I don't know'. This is your brain trying to keep you from feeling uncomfortable. Ask yourself: what if I needed to write down *something, or anything,* rather than 'I don't know'? There are no right or wrong things to write down.

Another thing you can do is a brain dump. This is exactly how it sounds: just dump all the thoughts in your head onto a piece of paper or the journalling page (or your screen or voice memo, etc.). Even if the thought doesn't relate to money, jot it down. This practice will help you get comfortable with seeing your thoughts written down.

Brain motivation factors

- **Interest:** Really getting into your deep (or shallow!) thoughts about money can be engaging, especially as you will probably discover new things about yourself along the way.
- **Challenge:** Make it a daily or weekly goal to sit down with your journal.

SIDEQUEST

Journal prompts to get you going

If you haven't journalled before, here are some prompts you can use to get started.

- What are three emotions I often feel when I think about money? Why do I think I feel this way?
- What is my earliest memory of money, and how does it influence my current beliefs or behaviours?

(continued)

- What financial habits have I tried in the past? Which ones worked, and which didn't?
- How do I typically react to unexpected expenses or financial surprises? How do I feel, and what do I do?
- What's one action I could take to feel more in control of my cash flow?
- What's a spending decision I made recently that made me feel really proud? Why?
- What's one area where I feel like money 'disappears'? How could I be better at tracking money in that area?
- If money weren't an obstacle, what would I spend more on? Less on?
- What financial goal excites me the most right now? What's one small step I can take towards it?
- How do I typically plan for future expenses, and how could I simplify the process?
- What would my ideal monthly budget look like? How does it align with my current spending?
- How does my ADHD affect the way I handle or think about money? What's one way I can work *with* my brain instead of against it?
- What is a financial strength I have because of my ADHD (e.g. creativity, hyperfocus)? How can I lean into that more?
- How does impulsive spending show up in my life? What strategies could help me pause before I spend?
- When I feel overwhelmed by financial tasks, what helps me calm down and get back on track?
- When I look back a year from now, what's one financial habit I want to have improved in that time?
- What's one thing about my financial situation that's better than I give myself credit for?

> - What would financial freedom feel like for me?
> - What's one kind understanding message I want to remind myself about money today?

Strategy: Gamifying

Gamifying, also called **gamification**, is when we use the elements and principles of game design to make other activities more engaging.

Gamifying takes advantage of things like our brain's desire to compete (against others or against ourselves) and achieve goals and milestones (e.g. completing a task or gaining points).

This strategy can be used for good or for evil. For example, corporations also use gamifying in advertising to encourage you to keep spending, and apps use it to keep you playing and scrolling.

So how can we gamify our finances for good, you ask? Great question. Here are a few ways.

Savings challenges

You may have seen savings challenges before. They are fun targets that have graphs to fill in or little images to colour in, helping you to track your savings progress and keep focused on it. (I've shared some in the next chapter.) You choose your savings goal, calculate the incremental amount you need to save into weeks or months, and then assign each item that dollar amount. Once you have saved the amount for one item fill in the graph or colour in the image.

Debt challenges

Debt challenges are pretty much the same as the savings challenges, but debt pay-down style! Each graph or image represents an amount you have put towards your debt, and you can visually watch your debt reduce. Don't underestimate the gratification your brain can get from the visuals.

(See the next chapter for worksheets you can use, and more on debt and savings generally.)

Quick wins

A quick win could be either a small savings goal or a small debt you want to quickly pay down. You might even choose one thing to budget for and make that your goal over the next month. Set a reasonable target amount and a timeframe.

Achieving a short-term goal like this has a couple of benefits:

- It shows your brain you can actually do the thing you perceive to be hard.
- It lights up the reward centre of your brain, giving you some dopamine, which makes you want to do the thing over and over again!

Reward yourself

OK, so you don't want this to go the 'wrong' way, right?! There's a fine balance between allowing yourself a reward as motivation — or going overboard and undoing all the hard work you have done.

Rewards can be low-cost, free, or even something you have been saving for.

Some reward ideas include:

- your favourite takeaway
- dinner with a friend
- a new book you have been wanting to read
- a night in with your favourite movie and snacks.

You get the idea. What do you absolutely love to do that you can put in as a reward for sticking to your grocery budget for the month? Or smashing down a small debt?

If you have a larger debt or savings goal, or even if you stuck to your budget for six months, you can give yourself small rewards along the way. Giving yourself something to look forward to will help keep you interested and keep your brain in the game.

Brain motivation factors

Gamifying can fall into all four motivation categories, so it's a winner!

- ☆ **Novelty:** Using different kinds of challenges and rewards for different money tasks keeps things interesting.
- 🎧 **Interest:** Turning a financial task into a more fun activity (like colouring in a savings or debt challenge) helps to keep you engaged and excited about it.
- △ **Challenge:** Gamifying lets you set specific goals *and* rewards for a task. Very satisfying.
- ⏰ **Urgency:** Setting quick wins for the immediate future helps create a sense of urgency around achieving that goal.

Strategy: Coaching and consulting

Sometimes we cannot get out of our own heads. Sometimes we need a second pair of eyes go over what we're working on to help us make it make sense.

This is where coaching and consulting come into play. Both do different things, so let's run through it.

- A **coach** is someone who helps you build financial management skills, navigate your emotions around money, and set and achieve goals.
- A **consultant** (like a financial advisor or an accountant) can look at your finances, help you make a plan and do the calculations for you. They can look at the big picture and help you work your way through the mess that your finances might be in.

It is most important you find someone you click with. But it is also a good idea to seek out someone who has an understanding of neurodivergence — and how it relates to your relationship with and your understanding of money.

Brain motivation factors

- 🎧 **Interest:** Personalised guidance that is tailored to your own goals and needs can be really motivating.

Strategy: Therapy

Oof, now we are getting deep. If you have some deep-rooted financial behaviours from the past, or financial trauma, this is where a therapist comes in.

A therapist can work with you to move through your past and current trauma or behaviours — something you may not be able to do on your own.

Remember: there's nothing wrong with asking for help when you need it. Therapy and coaching are amazing for ADHD brains (I told you I'd say it again!), whether you need financial therapy or not.

Did you know a therapist can even work closely with your coach or consultant? (With your permission, of course!)

If you're looking to find a good therapist, you can speak to your GP for recommendations. You can also ask around for recommendations from people like those in your support group or in online communities like ADHD Money.

Brain motivation factors

- 🔺 **Challenge:** Therapy isn't always easy, but addressing and overcoming your emotional barriers to money is a challenge worth embracing — and one that can be deeply rewarding.

- 🎧 **Interest:** What's more interesting to us than ... ourselves? Therapy can help you gain a new understanding and appreciation for yourself as a person.

Strategy: Habit stacking

You might remember the term 'habit stacking' from chapter 4, where we went through some tips for tracking your expenses. Well, this strategy can be used for other money tasks too, and I've seen it work for a lot of my clients.

Habit stacking involves pairing a task that you need or want to do with a habit you *already* do and enjoy.

By combining a money task with something else you do regularly, you make that task easier to remember and can do it more consistently too.

You might even start to look forward to managing your money this way, because you can pair what seems like a chore with a 'reward', or something else you like or find satisfying.

Step 1: Identify some habits that are already part of your daily or weekly routine

For example, do you:

- brush your teeth every night
- take a coffee break every morning
- make time to read a book you like on most weekends
- relax with a sleepy tea every night before bed
- work out at the gym or go for a run regularly
- get Friday-night takeaways most weeks?

As we know, the ADHD brain isn't always good with consistency and routine. And that's OK.

The trick here is to find the little habits you *do* already have — the ones that come naturally to you. Then, start small.

Step 2: During or immediately after your existing habit, add the new task

- After you brush your teeth at night, take five minutes to track your expenses from that day.
- On your morning coffee break, take one minute to check your bank balance.
- Before you order your Friday-night takeaways, fill in your progress on your savings or debt challenge.

You can also use visual cues to help you remember to stack. For example, if you want to start checking your bank balance with your morning coffee, stick a reminder on the coffee maker or the cupboard where your coffee cups live.

Again, the key is to find what already works for you and start small. The habit might be as simple as using your favourite pen when you sit down to do a worksheet or track your expenses.

And if you find yourself getting bored with the new routine, you can adjust the habits that you stack — don't be afraid to switch it up.

Brain motivation factors

- 🎧 **Interest:** Pairing a money task with a regular habit you already enjoy can help make it feel more fun and rewarding.
- ✨ **Novelty:** Changing how and where you do a task can help it feel fresh and different.

Cheat sheet: Strategies to keep things new and shiny

Body doubling	Working alongside another person to complete a task.
	Motivation factors: 🎧 **Interest:** A social connection can help you to feel more supported and engaged, rather than isolated or anxious. ⚠ **Challenge:** Having another person present can increase our sense of accountability and even create a positive sense of peer pressure. (You want to work as well as they do.)
Joining a support group	Find an existing group — or create your own with friends.
	Motivation factors: 🎧 **Interest:** Sharing our experiences with others is highly engaging, especially if you're a social person. ✨ **Novelty:** Hearing other people's perspectives and getting new ideas from them can keep things fresh.
Journalling	Daily or weekly, use whatever format works for you (e.g. pen and paper, a digital format or voice recording), record your thoughts and feelings about money.
	Motivation factors: 🎧 **Interest:** Really getting into your deep (or shallow!) thoughts about money can be engaging, especially as you will probably discover new things about yourself along the way. ⚠ **Challenge:** Make it a daily or weekly goal to sit down with your journal.

(continued)

Gamify	Use principles from game design to bring the fun.
	Motivation factors: ✦ **Novelty:** Using different kinds of challenges and rewards keeps things interesting. 🎧 **Interest:** Turning a financial task into a fun activity (like colouring in a savings or debt challenge) helps to keep you engaged and excited about it. ⚠ **Challenge:** Gamifying lets you set specific goals and rewards for a task. Very satisfying. ⏰ **Urgency:** Setting quick wins for the immediate future helps to create a sense of urgency around achieving that goal.
Coaching and consulting	Get expert advice when you need it, from someone who works with money all the time.
	Motivation factors: 🎧 **Interest:** Personalised guidance that is tailored to your own goals and needs can be really motivating.
Therapy	A therapist can help you process your thoughts and feelings about money. You can find one who works specifically with ADHD clients through your GP or by word of mouth.
	Motivation factors: ⚠ **Challenge:** Therapy isn't always easy, but addressing and overcoming your emotional barriers to money is a challenge worth embracing — and one that can be deeply rewarding. 🎧 **Interest:** What's more interesting to us than … ourselves? Therapy can help you gain a new understanding and appreciation for yourself as a person.

Habit stacking	Combine a habit you already have with a money task to create a new routine.
	Motivation factors: 🎧 **Interest:** Pairing a money task with a regular habit you already enjoy can help make it feel more fun and rewarding. ✨ **Novelty:** Changing how and where you do a task can help it feel fresh and different.

CHALLENGE
Your financial toolbox

Ok, now it's your turn to do some brainstorming.

- Are some of the strategies outlined in this chapter things you can put into your toolbox?
- Are there other techniques or tools that we haven't covered that you think might help you?

Use the following worksheet to brainstorm strategies and tools you'd like to try. As usual, I've filled out an example for you — but keep in mind, you probably don't want to try all these things at once. That's a good way to get overwhelmed. Instead, create your toolbox, then start by checking off just one or two of the tools you want to try.

Some helpful notes on creating your toolbox:

- Tools help, until they don't. Don't be afraid to switch it up when you need to. If you have a few strategies in your toolbox, but you want to try something new sometimes, go for it! Switching it up can also help keep up the novelty so you don't get bored.

- Your tools and strategies only have to make sense to you. This is *your* toolbox. Not your friend's or another ADHDer's. Make it your own.

- You don't have to fill in all the blank lines in the worksheet. If you are feeling overwhelmed at even the thought of doing this, then choose just one thing. You can add onto it if or when you feel ready.

My financial toolbox

IDEAS TO HELP KEEP THE NOVELTY ALIVE

- [ ] Set a $500 savings challenge (use a worksheet from chapter 7)
- [ ] Pay down a small debt ($100 I owe Mum and Dad)
- [ ] Find a coach and try a session
- [ ] Find an accountant and have a consult
- [ ] Ask support group and GP for recommendations for a therapist
- [ ] Commit to trying 3 x therapy sessions to start
- [ ] Find a mindfulness meditation I like and try it once a day for a week
- [ ] Stick to my grocery budget for 1 month
- [ ] Call my electricity company for a better deal
- [ ] Call my bank about a better home loan rate
- [ ] Book in dinner with a friend as a reward for hitting one of my goals
- [ ] Save by having a movie night in instead of going out
- [ ] Body double with a friend to track last month's spending
- [ ] Get some support from an ADHD Facebook Group
- [ ] Book in a monthly money night with my partner
- [ ] Sell some things I don't need around the house (e.g. clothes I haven't worn in 2+ years)
- [ ] Journal my goals and ideas every day for two weeks — habit stack this with my nightly cup of tea

NOTES AND REMINDERS

1. Search to see if there are better interest rates for my mortgage.
2. Book in a body doubling session to go through my bank transactions.

My financial toolbox

IDEAS TO HELP KEEP THE NOVELTY ALIVE

- [ ]
- [ ]
- [ ]
- [ ]
- [ ]
- [ ]
- [ ]
- [ ]
- [ ]
- [ ]
- [ ]
- [ ]
- [ ]
- [ ]
- [ ]
- [ ]
- [ ]
- [ ]

NOTES AND REMINDERS

Tools help, until they don't. Don't be afraid to switch it up when you need to.

CHAPTER 7
Saving Money and Paying Off Debt

In this chapter we get into ...

- How savings and debt can make you feel
- Why saving can be such a challenge with ADHD
- Scaffolding (i.e. tools and strategies) that can make saving easier
- How to use a savings challenge
- Good debt, bad debt, and why these labels aren't so helpful
- Two strategies for paying off debt:
    - The snowball method
    - The avalanche method
- How to use a debt challenge to make those strategies even easier
- Some final tips for keeping on top of debt

Less guilt, more scaffolding

If you've been reading this book chapter by chapter, I hope that by now you've realised there's more to financial wellness than just having a savings plan or curbing your impulsive spending. Your emotions, your mindset and your money are all interrelated.

When it comes to savings and debt, it's not as easy as saying 'just save money' or 'just pay off your debt', *especially* for an ADHDer.

Savings can feel like an elusive goal for those of us with ADHD. The urge for impulsive spending often takes precedence over the long-term benefits of saving, leading to a cycle of save and spend — or not saving at all.

That can also mean debt might accumulate quickly and unexpectedly.

Whether it's due to missed payments, high-interest credit cards or unplanned expenses, debt can lead to feelings of stress, shame and guilt. Which doesn't help our ADHD symptoms, right?

I'd like to offer some words of comfort: *there is no shame in being in debt*.

I know it certainly feels that way when we constantly read and hear how bad debt is.

Just like with anything to do with money, I lean away from labelling debt as *good* or *bad*. Sure, there is debt that is better to have than other debt (e.g. investment or education debt over consumer debt). But the more we label our debt as *bad*, the more shame and guilt we feel.

And if our emotions create our actions, what actions do you think you might take if you feel a whole bunch of shame and guilt? Avoidance? Disassociation?

Similarly, if we label our debt as *good* debt, we may want to accumulate more of it, and that can result in an amount we struggle to pay off.

In this chapter, I will lead you through some insights and actionable steps you can take to help you save and/or pay off debt. The end goal? To develop healthier financial habits and achieve financial wellness with ADHD.

Saving money

If you have ever tried to save for a rainy day, or for an emergency fund, and you haven't been successful, then listen up!

Let's go through some of the challenges of saving with ADHD. Some of it we have already touched on in earlier chapters, so we won't dwell on them too much. But it's still helpful to revisit these topics — because you know how our beautiful brains are with remembering things!

Impulsivity

As we know, this is one of the hallmark traits of ADHD. Thinking about long-term consequences will not make us stop acting impulsively.

Examples:

- Doing the grocery shopping and buying a bunch of things that aren't on your list.
- Shopping for a gift for your partner, but buying one of those cool new headphones for yourself instead.
- Going out to lunch and spotting some new clothes in the window of a shop you can't help but go into.

If we keep spending impulsively like this, over time it can make saving our money that much harder. This might be something you are well versed in already, my ADHD friend.

And before someone tries to tell you that you just aren't trying hard enough or don't see the importance of saving money ... this is simply not true. You know how powerful that urge to spend impulsively can be.

Executive functioning

Planning, prioritising and following through on tasks is required to save successfully. That means: planning the budget, prioritising necessary expenses and following through on what you have planned out by saving.

But sometimes the planning can stop us in our tracks, and then nothing happens after that. Our executive dysfunction affects our ability to carry out these tasks. And our working memory can affect our ability to remember due dates for bills or other financial commitments.

Emotional spending

Emotional spending can really affect our ability to save money, whether it's through overspending, spending impulsively or social spending. Feeling stressed, tired, frustrated or even excited can all make us more prone to spend in ways that don't benefit us in the long run. Chapter 2 talks about this in detail (if you haven't read it yet or want a refresher).

The right scaffolding can make saving easier

But things like impulsivity, inability to plan and prioritise, and emotional spending are not the end of the world. With the right strategies, you can work with your brain to make saving money and paying off debt easier.

Remember: you are not bad with money. You just need to find what works for you.

So let's talk about some scaffolding to help us save money. From using your accounts in different ways and setting up automated payments, to making saving more visual and rewarding, the following strategies can help you get on top of your debt and start (or improve on) this elusive *saving* thing.

Set more specific financial goals

Saving without a goal can be really unmotivating. We need the *why*, or some other immediate feedback, to feel like saving money is actually important.

So, what are you saving *for*? Remember, your savings goals can be big or small, for example:

- a holiday (where?)
- a downpayment for a home
- a new smartphone
- Christmas presents
- school/university supplies
- your wedding
- starting your dream business
- a new pair of shoes
- your BFF's bachelorette weekend
- your favourite hobby (e.g. art supplies, wool for knitting, sports gear)
- money for a monthly date night
- a comfortable retirement
- a new air conditioner.

(Read chapter 8 if you need help with financial goal setting.)

We need the *why*, or some other immediate feedback, to feel like saving money is actually important.

Create specific savings accounts

When you have more specific savings goals, you can also get creative with *how* you save.

Transferring money to an account called 'savings' can be a bit boring. Not only that, but if there is nothing specific you are saving for, it can be difficult to resist transferring money out of your savings when you run short elsewhere.

What's one way to combat this? You can use different, specific savings accounts for different savings goals. These days, many banks will let you open more than one 'everyday' or 'savings' account to help manage your money.

A fun way to manage your savings accounts is to call each account something interesting. For example, if you are saving money for a holiday to Japan, call the savings account 'Off to Tokyo'. If you need to save money to buy a new car, you might call the account the 'Vroom-Vroom Vault'. An account specifically for impulse spending could be 'Fun Money' or 'Treat Yo'self'.

Here are some other examples of different targets and account names, to get your creativity flowing:

- Can't Touch This
- Safe to Spend
- Netflix and Chill
- Home Sweet Home
- Christmas Cash
- Dollars for Doggo
- Paris is Waiting
- Work Hard, Play Hard
- Bali Buckeroos
- Date Night Dollars

- Book Budget
- Disaster Plaster
- Santa's Secret Stash
- New Phone Funds.

You get the idea. Even if you can't rename the accounts in your banking app, you can always name your worksheets, trackers or money spreadsheet fun names like this.

Automate your savings

Setting up transfers from your everyday account to a savings account can help you put money aside regularly.

Now, I will admit I am neither here nor there with automation. Some ADHDers swear by it, but I advise to approach it with some caution. Automating savings transfers can be great to help you in terms of lightening the mental load around managing your finances. But if you choose to automate, you should still ensure you are across *how much* you've got saved. It's less 'set and forget' and more 'set and keep track of'.

Set rewards

This strategy goes back to that interest-based nervous system!

Our brain likes rewards. So set yourself a timeframe for your saving, with milestones along the way, and let yourself celebrate when you reach each milestone.

You could set aside a small amount of money to reward yourself with a little splurge for sticking to your goal.

But you don't have to use a monetary reward. You could also reward yourself with something like personal time, a (free or low-cost) social activity you enjoy, making your favourite meal, doing some self-care at home, listening to your favourite music or watching your favourite show.

Make it visual

You've probably heard the saying 'out of sight, out of mind,' and this is especially true with ADHD. The more we can see something, the more we keep that thing front of mind.

Keep your savings goals where you can see them, and revisit them often to remind yourself why you are saving. For example, you could:

- Leave a savings challenge on your desk for colouring in regularly.
- Put up a whiteboard or cork board with words and pictures that remind you of your goals.
- Leave sticky notes in helpful places around your house.
- Frame a photo that reminds you of your goal.
- Put a totem or small object that reminds you of your goal on your bedside table, where you'll see it every night and every morning.
- Make a vision board and use it as your phone background.

Savings challenges

Savings challenges can be a fun way to gamify your savings. (You might remember that we also touched on these in chapter 6.)

A visual savings challenge consists of a worksheet with a thermometer, a graph or lots of little pictures. You might also have a bank or an app that can visually show you your progress.

Here's how it works:

- **Step 1:** Choose your savings goal.
- **Step 2:** Calculate how much money you need to reach that goal.
- **Step 3:** Break that total amount down into smaller, more achievable increments. For example, how much would you need to save every day, every week or every month to get to the total?

- **Step 4:** Assign that dollar amount to each of the small pictures or segments on the worksheet. Each picture now represents one smaller savings goal that will eventually add up to your total.

- **Step 5:** Every time you successfully save that smaller amount, you get to colour in one picture.

It can help to keep your savings challenge somewhere you will see it often, or stack it with another habit (see chapter 6 again for a refresher on habit stacking).

A savings challenge plays into our sense of challenge (a clear, defined goal we want to achieve) and reward (as we colour it in, we get to see our progress visually).

As you can see from the examples on the next pages, you can pick an image for your challenge that represents your specific savings goal, which also helps to keep that end reward top of mind.

I've included one thermometer example in this book but lots of little pictures is my favourite style of savings challenge, because it reminds me what I'm saving for.

Keep your savings goals where you can see them, and revisit them often to remind yourself *why* you are saving.

CHALLENGE
Try a savings challenge

Following the instructions, and using one of the worksheets on the following pages, start your own personal savings challenge.

It can be a good idea to start small. That might be something like saving money to buy a birthday present for a loved one, to go on a weekend away or, even, simply for your next electricity bill.

What's a savings goal you'd like to achieve in the near future? Something you could do in the next few days, weeks or months?

Savings challenge

Saving for		Start date	
Amount		End date	

$_____ $_____ $_____ $_____

$_____ $_____ $_____ $_____

$_____ $_____ $_____ $_____

$_____ $_____ $_____ $_____

Savings challenge

Saving for	
Amount	

Start date	
End date	

$_____ $_____ $_____
$_____ $_____ $_____
$_____ $_____ $_____
$_____ $_____ $_____
   $_____ $_____

Savings challenge

Saving for		Start date	
Amount		End date	

Savings challenge

Saving for		Start date	
Amount		End date	

Savings challenge

Saving for		Start date	
Amount		End date	

$____ $____ $____ $____

$____ $____ $____ $____

$____ $____ $____ $____

$____ $____ $____ $____

Navigating debt

So now you've got some strategies that can help you save. But it might be that the first thing you are setting aside money for with your savings goals is to pay off a debt.

Debt is not all the same.

- Sometimes we rack up debt because of our choices.
- Sometimes we get into debt because we don't have the financial literacy we need at the time.
- Sometimes we have debt because we have needs but don't have the cash flow available.

Sometimes debt is necessary. And sometimes the debt you have may have saved your life at the time. Everyone has a different reason for being in debt, and it isn't always for frivolous reasons like we are led to believe.

You might have heard about 'good' and 'bad' debt. Generally, consumer debt (things like credit card debt or car payments) is considered bad. Education (like student loans) and investment debt (like your mortgage) are considered better. However, as we acknowledged above, categorising debt this way, as *good* and *bad*, often just adds to the shame we feel in having it.

In an ideal world, we wouldn't get into debt. If only we could cash flow everything!

But I'm going to tell you a secret. *Even wealthy people have debt.* They just know how to leverage it, rather than be afraid of it.

The main categories of debt

Categories of debt	Examples
Consumer debt	Personal loans
	Buy Now Pay Later
	Credit cards
	Car loans
Education debt	University
	Postgraduate or additional qualifications
Investment debt	Property
	Shares
	Private equity

Even wealthy people have debt. They just know how to leverage it, rather than be afraid of it.

Ways to pay off debt

There really isn't a right or wrong way to pay off debt. Ultimately, you just want to pay it off!

Ideally, you want to minimise the interest paid on larger debts. But sometimes it makes more sense to just pay down your smallest debt first, to get the dopamine hit and prove to yourself that you can do it. That can give you the motivation to keep going and tackle a bigger debt.

There are two popular methods for paying off debt:

- the **snowball method**
- the **avalanche method**.

Let's take a quick look at both of them.

CHALLENGE
Try a debt challenge

As with saving, it can be really helpful to pair paying off debt with a visual aid.

Similar to a savings challenge, you can set yourself a debt challenge. That is, you can use a colouring worksheet, like those on the following pages, to track your success in paying down a debt. As with saving money, using a worksheet to track your debt payments will help you keep the end goal in sight and create a sense of reward and achievement along the way.

Keep the worksheet somewhere you can see it often.

Snowball method

I find the snowball method an especially good strategy for people with ADHD. It involves paying off the smallest debt first, which then 'snowballs' into paying off the bigger debts. Once we get a taste of paying off a debt successfully, we can feel more confident and more motivated to keep going.

This method is pretty simple. Here's how to get started:

- List all your debts.
- Order them by amount starting from the smallest debt to the largest.
- Take the smallest debt.
- Budget a set amount that you will pay towards this smallest debt each pay cycle.
- Use a debt challenge worksheet (like the one on the next page) to track your progress.

Debt challenge worksheet

Debt		Amount	$_____
Creditor		Account No.	
Minimum payment	$_____	Interest rate	____%
Due date	__/__/____	Goal payoff date	__/__/____

Date	Amount	Balance	Notes

$__ 100%
$__ 95%
$__ 90%
$__ 85%
$__ 80%
$__ 75%
$__ 70%
$__ 65%
$__ 60%
$__ 55%
$__ 50%
$__ 45%
$__ 40%
$__ 35%
$__ 30%
$__ 25%
$__ 20%
$__ 15%
$__ 10%
$__ 5%
$__ 0%

Avalanche method

This second method for paying off debt is a good strategy if you have debts with high interest rates or you prefer to save on the amount of interest you pay over time.

The avalanche method involves paying the debts with the highest interest rates first.

As with the snowball method, it's pretty straightforward. Here's how it works:

1. List all your debts. Include the associated interest rate for each one.
2. Order your debts from the highest interest rate to the lowest.
3. Take the debt with the highest interest rate.
4. Budget a set amount of money you aim to pay off with each pay cycle.
5. Use a debt challenge worksheet to track your progress.

Debt challenge worksheet

Debt		Amount	$_____
Creditor		Account No.	
Minimum payment	$_____	Interest rate	____%
Due date	__/__/___	Goal payoff date	__/__/___

Date	Amount	Balance	Notes

$ 100%
$ 95%
$ 90%
$ 85%
$ 80%
$ 75%
$ 70%
$ 65%
$ 60%
$ 55%
$ 50%
$ 45%
$ 40%
$ 35%
$ 30%
$ 25%
$ 20%
$ 15%
$ 10%
$ 5%
$ 0%

Some final tips for paying off your debt

Now you're armed with some strategies you can try to tackle your debt and start saving.

There are a few things you can do to help with paying off what you owe and to reach your goal steadily and successfully. Here are some final tips you can draw on when it comes to keeping on top of debt.

Other tips to keep on top of debt

It's a good idea to …	For example …	Because you'll …
Keep paying all the minimum payments on each of your debts.	Before your monthly billing cycle is due.	Avoid late fees and penalties. Yay.
Allocate extra payments where you can.	When you receive some extra money, like a tax refund or bonus.	Reduce your debt faster.
Allocate extra payments to the debts with the highest interest rates when following the avalanche method.	When you receive some extra money, like a tax refund or bonus.	Reduce the total interest you'll pay over time, saving you money in the long term.
Allocate extra payments to the debts with the lowest balance when following the snowball method.	When you receive some extra money, like a tax refund or bonus.	Enjoy quick wins, boosting your motivation and confidence.

It's a good idea to…	For example…	Because you'll…
Celebrate your wins!	When you've successfully stuck to the amount you planned to pay off this pay day, paid off a debt in full or made an 'extra' payment.	Use a sense of reward to positively reinforce that you can keep going and you can do this. Go you!
Adjust as you need.	When things change, you should review your financial situation to ensure you can still budget for the payment amounts you have allocated to each debt. (Or if you can pay more!)	Give yourself flexibility to adapt to changes and still stay on track.

CHAPTER 8
Setting Achievable Goals

In this chapter we get into ...

- Why setting and following through on goals can be hard
- Why your goals might not look like everyone else's goals
- How to set more sustainable, achievable goals using the BRAVE method

Getting where you want to go

Many of us have financial goals. Whether it's wanting to save for a holiday, buy a house, get out of debt or get a pay rise at work, goals can take some hardcore executive functioning to plan and implement.

When it comes to goal setting, a neurotypical person can focus on the big picture. Think of goal setting for a holiday or buying a house; these things usually aren't just one goal, even though they seem like it. There are lots of little steps you have to take and smaller goals that you have to achieve on the way. That's not so simple for the ADHD brain.

These particular examples are also long-term goals, so you have to stay focused on your goal for months or even years to make it happen. Also not so easy for us.

However, even a short-term goal can wreak havoc on a neurodivergent brain that struggles with executive functioning. This is why you may have found that when you have set goals in the past, you gave up on them quickly or struggled to see them through and achieve the goal.

A well-known way to set goals is setting **SMART goals**, which stands for **s**pecific, **m**easurable, **a**ttainable, **r**ealistic and **t**ime based. This is a great way to set goals, and it might work for you.

However, as ADHDers struggle with decision making, time blindness and overwhelm, I started to wonder if there is a better way for our neurodivergent brains to set goals.

The BRAVE method

I don't know about you, but even hearing the word SMART for goal setting makes me think of a typical, socially normal goal that may not suit my interests or my lifestyle.

So I had a think about what we needed to do when it came to goal setting. I knew it needed to play into our interests, and be simple and flexible. I came up with what I call the BRAVE method.

BRAVE stands for:

1. **B**reak down the steps
2. **R**ealistic
3. **A**ttractive
4. **V**alues based
5. **E**mpowered

In this chapter, we'll run through what each of these key points means — and how you can put them together to create a goal that is easier for you to stick with and achieve.

Make your goals ... BRAVE

B — **Break down**
How will you break down your goal into actionable steps?

R — **Realistic**
Is it realistic to your current lifestyle and finances?

A — **Attractive**
Is this your goal and something you actually want to achieve?

V — **Values based**
Is it in line with your values?

E — **Empowered**
Do you feel empowered to achieve your goal?

1. Break down the steps

As I mentioned above, typical goal setting often seems like it's aimed at one goal. For example:

- Save for a house deposit.
- Go on a holiday.
- Save for a wedding.
- Buy a new car.

But these big goals actually have lots of little steps you have to follow along the way.

Take saving for a house deposit. If you need to save $60 000, that is quite a large amount! You might feel a rush of dopamine from the excitement of picturing yourself saving up that amount and then buying your very own property. But unfortunately that initial rush can quickly be overtaken by overwhelm, maybe before you have even really started.

So what do we do? Rather than shy away from setting the goal in the first place, breaking down the steps involved in this goal can be helpful. This also helps to combat any feelings of overwhelm.

So, maybe your goal *isn't* to save $60 000 for a house deposit. Maybe your first goal is to save $10 000. Or even just $5000. Once you get that amount saved, you can move on and even increase your next savings goal.

The long-term timeline doesn't need to change. You can still aim to save a house deposit in, say, five years' time. You are simply breaking up the huge total amount of money into smaller, more manageable chunks.

And much like the snowball method of paying off debt, once you get that taste of having saved for your first money goal, you will become empowered to keep going. Because now you know you can do it.

2. Realistic

OK, this might sound a bit obvious, but setting *realistic* goals is all about being ... well, realistic. In other words: be practical. Sometimes that means being really honest with yourself. Sometimes it means considering the most important outside factors, those beyond your control.

A goal is realistic if:

- you can afford it
- you have the non-financial means (like the knowledge, skills or connections to make it happen)
- it's something you *want* to do or value.

For example, if you really want a house that is out of your price range, is it realistic to try to save for the deposit for it? Or say you really want to save for holiday to go overseas for two months. Can you realistically get that amount of time off work? It may be more realistic to plan for a shorter holiday.

You'll find setting and pursuing your goals a lot easier if the goal is something you know you can take the practical steps to achieve. (We'll come back to values shortly: they're the V in BRAVE.)

3. Attractive

Remember our interest-based nervous system? Well, we must actually *want* to achieve the goals we are setting. In other words, your goal should be something that's attractive to you personally.

This step is your reminder to check in with whether the goal you're setting is something you really *want* to do — and not just something you think you *should* do. For example, many people want to buy a house. But some don't. If you are in the group that doesn't, then trying to achieve this goal might just be a bit more difficult.

Another way to view attractive goals is to set your goal in a way that it doesn't seem so big and scary. If you go from no goal setting at all to a huge one-year goal, that goal maybe doesn't seem so attractive. This is because our brains struggle to plan that far in advance.

To combat this, you can set shorter term goals. By that I mean set a small goal for one month. Once that feels good and comfortable, stretch it out a bit. (Hopefully, if you're breaking down the steps, you've already considered this.)

4. Values Based

In chapter 4, you started working out your financial values. Whip them back out, or head to page 115 to do this exercise, because knowing your values will come in handy for this part of your goal setting.

By understanding your core personal values, you can create a more purposeful relationship with your money and align your financial goals with what matters most to you. When our goals align with our values, it's easier to feel persistent and stay motivated about achieving them.

For example, you might value:

- family
- freedom
- security
- personal development
- giving to others
- education
- career
- mental health
- good food
- fun/lifestyle
- luxury
- holidays/travel.

If your end goal aligns with your values, then it's going to be more attractive (the A in BRAVE), and therefore easier to stay motivated about. If your goal doesn't align with your values, then it's going to be harder to achieve. For example, if you don't value travelling, why set a goal to travel to all these different places? If you don't value renting, then maybe it's time to start looking at your purchasing options.

5. Empowered

Your goals should make you feel empowered. Meaning you should feel confident and able to reach the goal you want to set for yourself.

Making sure your goal is realistic, attractive and values based (steps 2–4) will help with this. If your goal is something you know you can realistically achieve, and you really want to achieve it, then you're already going to feel more empowered.

Remember the example in the first step, with the $60 000 house deposit? If all you can see is a huge number in front of you — and you ultimately struggle to put the money aside — you won't feel empowered to keep going. And you definitely won't feel empowered to set other new goals.

How else can you feel empowered along the way to your goal? Rewards can be good.

What could your reward be for ticking off your first goal? Perhaps:

- a book you've had your eye on
- meeting a friend for a nice long hike
- heading out to a venue you've been wanting to try.

Rewards do not need to be monetary, nor do they need to be extravagant. They can be just something small you give yourself for taking a huge step towards your financial wellbeing. Remember to reward yourself and enjoy the journey, rather than just keeping your eyes set on the destination.

CHALLENGE
Set a BRAVE goal

Now that we've gone through the BRAVE method in detail, I'd love for you to give it a go.

Remember, your goal doesn't have to be a six- or 12-month target. Can it be? Absolutely! But if that freaks you out, then start with a month. Start with a week, even.

You can even apply the following worksheet to micro goals, like how many times you will go to the gym this week.

Set a BRAVE goal

MY GOAL
Save $15 000 for a holiday in 12 months' time

WHY I WANT TO ACHIEVE THIS
I've always wanted to go to France. There are things there I really want to experience and see (like the Louvre, the Eiffel Tower and Notre Dame) and do (like eat fancy French pastries).

IS IT A BRAVE GOAL?

B: Break down the steps	Yes, I can break down the steps. For example, save in smaller amounts, find accommodation that fits my budget, research flights.
R: Realistic	Yes, I can afford it, and I'll have enough holiday time owed at work.
A: Attractive	Yes, I really want to go overseas. I learned French in school and really want to practise it at last. I've always wanted to see the artworks in the Louvre.
V: Values based	Yes, travelling is one of my values.
E: Empowered	Yes, I feel empowered because this goal is realistic, attractive and values based. I can set smaller goals along the way and give myself rewards to help me get there.

HOW WILL I KEEP ON TRACK? WHAT SAVINGS STRATEGIES CAN I USE?	HOW WILL I MONITOR MY PROGRESS?
I will track my progress with a printable savings tracker and tick off each increment on the way (visualise, gamify).	I'll set a specific amount to save each quarter, then check in at the end of each period.

HOW I WILL GET TO MY GOAL

Date	Tasks or financial breakdown	✓
31 March	Save $3750 ($290 per week).	
30 June	Save $3750 ($290 per week).	
30 September	Save $3750 ($290 per week).	
31 December	Save $3750 ($290 per week).	
Tax time	I may get a tax refund I can save as a buffer.	
September	I'm due a bonus at work; I can save this if I have not reached savings my goal.	

Set a BRAVE goal

MY GOAL

WHY I WANT TO ACHIEVE THIS

IS IT A BRAVE GOAL?

B: Break down the steps	
R: Realistic	
A: Attractive	
V: Values based	
E: Empowered	

HOW WILL I KEEP ON TRACK? WHAT SAVINGS STRATEGIES CAN I USE?	HOW WILL I MONITOR MY PROGRESS?

HOW I WILL GET TO MY GOAL

Date	Tasks or financial breakdown	✓

CHAPTER 9

Frequently Asked Questions

In this chapter we get into ...

- Answers to some of the most common questions I get asked about ADHD and money
- Tips for where to look throughout this book for more info and advice on each topic
- A couple of extra money admin things

The answers you're looking for — well, some of them!

I've worked with many ADHDers in my time, and many of the same questions pop up. Whether I am working with someone one-on-one or presenting a webinar, I often get asked the same questions about money, from budgeting and expense tracking to savings and debt.

So let's run through the common issues that ADHDers face with money management, and hopefully I'll answer some of your questions too.

I've divided these questions into some key categories:

- money emotions
- budgeting
- spending
- saving
- expenses and debt
- money admin.

Where applicable, I've also referenced a chapter where you can read more about the answer. This might be especially helpful if you're not reading the book in order — you've may even have started here.

Money emotions

Why do I get overwhelmed every time I think about my finances?

Managing money involves a lot of planning, organising and decision making. We can create coping mechanisms such as being avoidant or only looking at our money in an emergency. This can be especially true if we have a lot going on in other areas of our lives. And that leaves less mental capacity for financial management.

Chapters 2 and 3 will help you here.

How can I build better financial habits when I struggle with consistency?

Scrap the idea of what consistency means. ADHDers struggle to be *typically* consistent. But your version of being consistent could be *persistence* instead.

For example, typical consistency might look like someone checking their money once a week on a Sunday night. For you, it could mean you don't look at your finances for two weeks, then you check them every week ... then maybe leave it for three weeks before coming back to it again.

There is no shame in this, so resist the urge to shame yourself into a routine that might not be realistic for you. Looking at your finances with the above routine is better than not looking at them at all!

Why do I find it hard to prioritise financial responsibilities over other tasks?

This has everything to do with our executive functioning! Prioritisation can be hard for our ADHD brain, especially when we haven't yet learned the skills to help us prioritise. It can also be boring; to prioritise what we need, as opposed to all those shiny new things we desire.

Head to chapters 1, 2 and 3 to read about it.

How can I manage the anxiety that comes with checking my bank balance?

Before sitting down to check your bank transactions, remember to use your go-to techniques for self-regulation and make sure your basic needs have been met. This can help with those feelings of anxiety you might have.

Head to chapters 2 and 3 for more information on this.

What if I fall off the wagon? How do I get back on?

Just hop straight back on ADHD friend! The longer you stay off, the harder it will be to move on. Remember, *be persistent over consistent*.

Budgeting

Why do I struggle with sticking to a budget, even though I know it's important?

ADHDers have an interest-based nervous system (as opposed to a consequence-based nervous system). Our brain doesn't respond to something just because it's 'important'. We tend to seek immediate rewards as opposed to focusing on the consequences.

The key is to find a way to make your finances interesting, rather than relying on them being important.

Head to chapter 5 to read up on sticking with your spending plan.

How can I make budgeting less boring, so I actually stick with it?

Here are a couple of suggestions:

- Make it manageable enough to fit in with your mental capacity. You might want to start with budgeting for just one or two areas of your money, for example food or impulsive spending.
- Make it colourful.
- Make it realistic.
- Reframe it — you tell your money what to do, rather than the other way around.

Head to chapters 3 and 5 to keep going with this.

What do I do when I have gone over budget?

Firstly, don't panic, and don't avoid! You're human, and this happens to all of us.

The best thing to do here is to see if you can make up the budget from another area.

From there, just move on. Try not to dwell on feeling guilty about it because, remember, your thoughts and emotions create your actions. More positive thoughts will create positive actions.

Check out chapter 3 for more on maintaining a positive mindset.

How do I budget when I have a varied income?

Find your minimum income for each month. This will involve you looking back at your income and seeing what the minimum might be, but it will give you a baseline to play with.

For example, if you can identify you earn at minimum $4000 per month, then budget off this amount. If you have months where this is higher, then you can think of that as a nice little bonus. Allocate the extra funds where they need to be allocated, like a savings goal, paying off debt or simply having a little extra cash flow.

Spending

I keep dipping into my savings for non-essential purchases. How can I stop?

Consider putting your savings somewhere that isn't as easily accessible. This could be a separate bank account without a debit card. Or you might have a savings account that has a waiting period before funds can be moved out.

You can also head to chapters 2 and 3 to do some work around overspending, emotional spending and your money mindset — these are so important for moving forward with your money.

How can I stop using retail therapy as a form of stress relief?

Find another way to increase your dopamine and relieve stress. Shopping might be an ingrained habit, but if you can think of other things you can do, it will benefit your financial future. For example, you could do some form of exercise you enjoy, do a puzzle or colouring or watch your favourite movie, just to name a few things.

And set boundaries around your phone if you find online shopping hard to curb.

How can I resist the urge to spend when I receive an unexpected windfall, like a bonus or tax refund?

This comes down to managing our impulsivity. Put some time in between wanting to spend and making a decision (head to chapter 2 to read tips on this). Or you could set a savings goal that takes into account how you'll spend 'extra' money (see chapter 7 for tips on savings goals).

Saving

I'm struggling to break down my financial goal into actionable steps. What can I do?

Head to chapter 8, where I help you break down your goals into actionable steps. You can also use a tool or app like Goblin Tools, which will help you break down goals and tasks.

Why do I struggle to set realistic financial goals?

Sometimes we can find it difficult to see what is realistic. For example, with time, we can over- or underestimate how long something will take. The same can be said for financial goals. We might know what we want, but breaking down the steps to get there can be hard — as can the timeline for the goal.

Not only that, but outside noise can sometimes make us want to set goals that aren't realistic either. They could be unrealistic in terms of timelines or your lifestyle. Buying a house is a good example of this. If you have a big goal like that, you'll want to assess whether it's realistic time wise, as well as if it fits the lifestyle you want to live.

The BRAVE method and worksheet in chapter 8 can help with realistic goal setting.

Expenses and debt

I tend to underestimate how much money I'll need. Why does this happen?

Planning ahead and estimating costs are part of executive functioning. This is where knowing your regular expenses can be of benefit. Knowing your past expenses can help you create a realistic idea of your money needs.

Chapters 4 and 5 can help with tracking your expenses and creating a personalised spending plan.

I have so many bills and expenses to manage. Why do I constantly forget to pay them on time?

Remembering deadlines is a real difficulty with ADHD. Not only that, but it requires planning and prioritising even to be able to automate a payment.

Even with an automated payment, it's easy to forget to have money in your account when the bill or expense is due. This is why I always recommend to check in with your money as often as you can.

I keep signing up for subscription services and forgetting about them. How do I stop this?

There are a few things you can do here:

- If you subscribe for a free trial via your phone app store, immediately go in and cancel the trial, right after you sign up. Usually this still gives you access to the whole free trial, and you don't have to remember to cancel it before the billing date. If you change your mind, you can always stop the cancellation.
- You can put a reminder in your calendar to cancel it before the billing date.
- Once a week or once a month, make a task to go into your bank account and do an audit of any subscriptions that have come out. From there, you can decide if you want to keep the subscription or cancel it. (And if you want to cancel it — do it right then and there.)

Why do I find it hard to plan for unexpected expenses like car repairs or medical bills?

This is where an emergency fund will come into play. Resist the urge for perfection; we cannot know what unexpected expenses will pop up during the year. If you just decide on an amount to put away for unexpected things, something is better than nothing!

Why is managing debt so difficult for me?

Debt management is another money task that involves having to create a plan to pay down the debt. And we know, planning can be difficult with ADHD. Head to chapter 7 to get help on coming up with a debt management/payoff plan.

Debt can also make us feel ashamed, and that can lead to avoidant behaviour around paying it off. Chapter 3 can help you address your mindset around money (and a therapist is another option for someone who can help you dive deep and work through those feelings too).

Money admin

Why do I find it difficult to file my taxes every year?

Ah! ADHDer, you are not alone on this. Taxes can be confusing and overwhelming, and not to mention the task of getting all your documents organised. It can be a nightmare for your ADHD brain.

One way to combat this is to come up with a system that you can continue throughout the year. For example, find somewhere you can store receipts and invoices digitally. Maybe even have a deadline with your accountant as to when you are going to file your taxes. This will help with accountability.

And don't feel you need to be a 'proper adult' and do your own taxes. Outsource, outsource, outsource! That's why accountants exist.

How do I keep from losing important financial documents?

Pick whether you are going to go digital or stick with paper. Having some paper and some digital just adds to the confusion.

Of course, there might be some things you need to have paper based even if you use a digital system (e.g. birth certificate).

For a paper-based system: pick out a fun filing folder to store all your documents inside. When you get something important, put it in there straight away. If you are going to put it in a hiding spot, put a hint for that secret spot in your phone notes (or similar) in case you forget.

For a digital system: choose your folder system, whether it is cloud based or local files on your computer. Decide if it's going to be filed by date (month, year) or by what the documents are (e.g. bank statements, tax). As with a paper system, as soon as you get something that you need to file, save it straight away.

Here's a rule I've heard that I really like: if it's going to take five minutes or less, do it straight away. Time yourself when you first start filing, so you will know if this is a five-minute (or less) task.

CONCLUSION
The dessert menu

In other words, this is the end. But I didn't want to leave you without a few final thoughts.

Whether you have read this book from beginning to end, or you've just read bits and pieces throughout, I hope you have picked up some new and interesting information. I hope you'll use the tips and worksheets here to help you start applying your incredible brain for managing your finances.

This might be the beginning of your financial journey. If it is, I encourage you to keep this book where you can see it so you can be motivated to keep picking it up. (I wanted the cover to be colourful so it looked inviting rather than scary!)

If you are not new to financial management, then I hope you have found some new activities to integrate into your current money-management tasks.

Your financial journey is uniquely yours. It will have its highs and lows, and everything in between. Every step you take, every time you pick up this book, every time you even *think* about your money is a step toward a brighter financial future.

You are not bad with money. You now have the resources and skills to create your abundant financial future.

You've got this.

Keep going.

The best is
yet to come.